God's Plan for His Church

A Manual for Church Planting and Church Renewal

Using Biblical Principles that Transcend Cultures and Time

Tim W. Bunn

11178 Huron Street, Suite 6
Northglenn, CO 80234-3343
303-232-4779
www.imdpress.com

God's Plan for His Church

A Manual for Church Planting and Church Renewal

Third Edition

Copyright © 2012 by IMD Press

Please send requests for information through our website:
www.imdpress.com

ISBN: 978-0-9833016-2-2
Printed in the United States of America

Illustrations by Christopher Esterly
Book design by Becky Hawley Design, LLC

11178 Huron Street, Suite 6
Northglenn, CO 80234-3343
303-232-4779
www.imdpress.com

What Others Are Saying

"The manual opened my eyes to the bitter reality that today's churches are off track from the biblical model. I learned to let the bible talk about the issue of church planting, and be more submissive to its authority and guidance. It was an eye opening resource for me."

Church Planter • Algeria

"This is a life changing book to those who would like to go back to the Word of God and apply the New Testament, especially the book of Acts. By applying these principles, we are experiencing revival in our families and churches in Zambia, and it is spreading to surrounding countries. Now the church is looking and acting more like the early church in Acts."

Pastor • Zambia, Africa

"I can say this manual is next to the Bible in relation to the church and its ministry. You ask how and why? I say, 'Because it takes the reader to the Bible itself to discover the supra-cultural and timeless biblical principles in establishing new churches.' This manual is a tool God can use to empower you to discover the process God wants you to follow for a growing and powerful church."

Church Planter • Myanmar

"God's Plan for His Church is being used in Cambodia to strengthen and grow the church. This manual is a powerful tool which contains biblical principles inspired by the living word of God which are applicable to personal life, family, church and mission especially to plant more new churches in new areas where none exist."

Chairman of National Christian Churches of Cambodia

"Going through the manual was the very important step in my life. I had a solid biblical and practical teaching through Acts book. It was a very fruitful time and as a fruit we put a strategy to plant three churches within three years; we started on January 1, 2012."

Church Planter • Egypt

God's Plan for His Church is a wonderful guide to compare today's church with the New Testament Church. It is completely non-biased and is based 100% on the Word of God. I highly recommend this book for personal use as well as for church group studies. I have seen this implemented first hand and have seen powerful results."

Church Planter • South America

"God's Plan for His Church Conference was one of the best I ever attended on the topic. It was a solid teaching built on the book of Acts and the principles used by Apostle Paul. It gave me a new perspective and approach in the areas of evangelism and witness for the Lord Jesus Christ."

Seminary Professor • Lebanon

"It is amazing how the Spirit of God is moving in a powerful way in restoring His Church after using this manual."

Church Planter • Bhutan

"The last fifteen years, I studied and applied this biblical philosophy in my life and ministry. When I used this manual in the ministry, I went from an educator to biblical church planter."

Church Planter • Karnataka, India

"By the end of the book each participant will have his own Bible-based, church planting strategy. The training method used to teach this manual is very simple. Each question presented makes the participants rely on the Holy Spirit to answer the truth from the Bible. The best thing about the manual is it is very practical."

Church Planter • Nepal

"God is using this manual to make a tremendous impact on the local churches in Vietnam. It is clear, complete and very useful in training church planters to establish new churches and to strengthen existing churches."

Church Planter • Vietnam

"This training manual has been a turning point in my ministry. After getting to know and understand what God wants from me as a church planter, I now follow the plan of God. He is building His church today from district to state and from state to other countries. This manual can help you discover that plan."

Church Planter • Bangladesh

"Wow, what a tool and based solely on the Word of God; one of the greatest tools outside the Bible. It cuts through all the junk man has added over 2,000 years and goes right back to those timeless principles of the New Testament church. God has worked in my life through this book and I have seen him work in the lives of many in Bhutan."

Church Planter • Bhutan

"God's Plan for His Church has been an eye opener to me, despite being in the ministry of saturation church planting for several years; little did I know that there is so much more in the book of Acts on church planting. This book unlike many good and theologically profound books, addresses the complex issues in the simplest form leading the local church planter to find answers from scripture through interactive study method."

Seminary Professor and Church Leader • Tamil Nadu, India

"God has used this manual to change my life and given the men around me a deeper root in the Scriptures. Our church is acting more like the one that the Scriptures talk about and many are blessed because of it."

Businessman and Pastor • North Carolina

"This manual could serve as a basic workbook for a church planting team wanting to plant a strong church with qualified leaders. The author teaches the need to multiply churches and how to develop a sustaining church planting movement. His chart showing accelerators and inhibitors to a church planting movement was extremely helpful."

Seminary Professor • Indiana

"This will be my second time going through *God's Plan for His Church* manual and I must say, it gets better and better! Why? Is it the manual itself? No, it is the effectiveness and simplicity of the material pointing the reader back to the scripture and focusing on the early church—how it started, how it grew, the structure, the family, how to handle discipline and develop leadership! What is most exciting is to see how this is spreading overseas—specifically in Southeast Asia and India, and now is starting to spread here in the US."

Leader • USA

"I studied through the whole manual and was extremely impressed with how it forces us to consider our lives and families based upon the Bible. Although seemingly a simple concept, the manual does not rely on conventional wisdom or the prevailing wind, but relies on God's proven principles that He established long ago that are still relevant for today."

Pastor • USA

"Just like the subtitle says, this manual uses God's timeless, supra-cultural principles for planting churches, and strengthening existing churches. There are no fads, gimmicks, catch-phrases, or anything that is going to be forgotten and gone in 10 years, just lesson after lesson of rightly dividing God's Word on how churches are to be operating as a body and how the individual believer is to live his life in God's Family."

Elder • USA

"Participants who work simultaneously through this training resource are most likely to discover God's biblical strategy for church planting as well as their individual direction for planting churches."

President, IMD International • Denver, Colorado

Contents and Progress Record

Put the date you completed the project/lesson on the line before the title.

CHAPTER 4
Our Challenge: Develop Faithful Leaders in the Church

CHAPTER 5
Our Challenge: Develop Strong Churches

CHAPTER 6
Our Challenge: Develop Ordered Churches   **133**

CHAPTER 7

Our Challenge: Develop a Church Planting and Renewal Strategy   229

Acknowledgments

I have developed this church planting manual to be used for the glory of our Lord and Savior, Jesus Christ! I am grateful for many church leaders who have been blessed by the previous editions and revisions as well as the many translations of the Church Planting Manual used throughout the world. I want to particularly thank my dear brothers, Sherman Driver and Phil Largent, who have come along side and made this manual possible through their wisdom, encouragement and partnership in the gospel.

I have been influenced over years of ministry by great men of God like Gene Getz and Roland Allen, so similarities to some of their materials may occur herein because "there is nothing new under the sun." I may have inadvertently used the material of others, but do not wish in any way to take away from the original author nor take credit or benefit for any such material. Any revenue from this material will not be used for the personal gain of the author or anyone else. All and any revenue will be used to provide translations around the world for our Lord's glory!

Tim Bunn

Foreword

Over the years, I have watched as God linked spiritually ready indigenous leaders with this training manual. The result in almost every such situation is a request to bring the training found in this manual to the ministry in the field. Humbly, we have watched and participated with the Lord in seeing multiple language editions of this manual placed into the hands and lives of key ministry leaders in many countries (the majority in the 10/40 window of South Asia). Tim Bunn has been captured by the Spirit of God and brought to develop this training manual out of decades of biblically based, multi-cultural ministry.

What you have in hand has been in use (though in earlier forms) for two decades by indigenous ministry leaders in Asia and South America. It is in use in the USA as well. Thus, the contents of this manual are not theoretical, but practical. God brought these principles to Tim who in turn has released them to leaders throughout the world. It is clearly the intention of Tim and IMD International that you learn and understand what is presented in this manual as well as implement the same in your ministry.

Let God lead you in applying the truths He brings to you through the use of this manual. He only is the source and power for building His church and expanding it to include all peoples around His earth. Since "faith comes by hearing and hearing by the Word of God," you can proceed with great faith in studying and applying the truths you will discover through the use of this manual. How can such a strong statement be made concerning faith? Because you are going to be led to open the Bible and let God show you Himself what He has to say about planting churches. Thus, faith in God will be the sure outcome of your study and the certain experience you have with God as you apply what He reveals to you in planting churches.

Surrender your all to the Lord. Apply yourself to completing all the lessons and projects in this manual. Interact with other disciples of Jesus as you walk through these lessons and projects. Plant churches according to His plan in the power of His Spirit. For herein, God is glorified.

A fellow servant of the Lord Jesus Christ and witness to these things,

Phil Largent, IMD International

Introduction

This manual is a complete tool to guide leaders and believers who desire to plant or renew a church. It is not training for ministry, rather training in ministry for those who sense God's call to church planting and renewal.

This manual is not theory or some Western or Eastern new teaching but a time-tested model, proven historically in Acts. It is not written to teach a new method or improve the old methods! A word of caution: it would be a travesty to become more biblical and neglect your relationship with Christ and the gift of the Holy Spirit.

If you sense this call, you may think that you must have a Bible College or a Seminary degree or financial support to establish a growing church. While there is absolutely nothing wrong with any of these, the Bible does give us a wonderful example of how the church originally began and was established without degrees or money. By following the example of Christ and the Apostles, in the power of the Holy Spirit, you can be successful in seeing a growing church planted and established.

Following these lessons will lead you to follow Paul's biblical example of laying the foundation and establishing growing communities of believers. This manual will lead you to develop a church planting and renewal strategy of your own following timeless and supra-cultural biblical principles which are simple, clear, and practical.

'Kingdom gain' is the desired outcome of the time you spend in this manual. To maximize your efforts in learning through the use of this manual, we offer you these important words of encouragement:

- Ask God to give you two or more faithful leaders with whom you can walk through these learning exercises.

- Intercede one for another constantly as you work through this training manual.

- Read, meditate, and complete every lesson in this manual. A useful *Progress Record* is located with the Table of Contents on pages 7-10 of this manual to help you keep track of your progress.

- Dialog with your ministry partners at the close or during regular intervals as you each work through this manual: listening to one another, praying with one another, and sharing your insights with one another.

- Trust the Holy Spirit for the boldness to accept what He is showing you and for the courage to change and act upon what He is teaching you.

- Apply promptly whatever truths God brings to you as you work through these lessons and projects. Avoid postponing what God leads you to do.

- Ask God to allow you to see more of His plans for your obedience in renewing churches—near and far—for His glory.

- Pass on to other disciples of Jesus the truths God is bringing to you through your meditation and application of His Word.

As you look to the Lord, be assured He desires to meet you, raise you up, further equip you, and empower and guide you with the Holy Spirit to plant and renew churches for His glory in your sphere of influence.

Chapter 1

OUR CHALLENGE
Return to the Scriptures

"I am constantly intrigued and challenged whenever I look at the logic and strategy of the young missionary church in the book of Acts, as I sought to "make disciples of all nations" (Matthew 28:19). Considering that the early church did not enjoy the numerical strength we have, or the technological advances we take for granted, one cannot but wonder how this small band of disciples and apostles made such a tremendous impact on their world. What was their secret? What can we learn from their strategy?"

David Zac Niringiye • Uganda, Africa

Discussion Questions: What do you think was the secret to the tremendous impact and expansion of the early church?

_____

_____

_____

_____

_____

What can we learn from the strategy of the early church? _____

_____

_____

_____

_____

_____

Paul's Biblical Example Introduced

Looking at the map below, how long did it take the gospel to spread from Jerusalem to Rome? Look again at the map below and tell me how many years it took Paul to complete all three of his missionary journeys? Amazing! It would be difficult to find any better model than the Apostle Paul in the work of establishing growing churches.

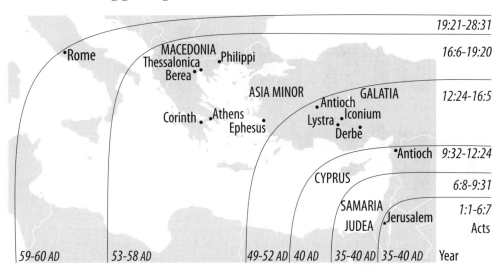

Yes, in just a little over ten years, Paul established the church in four provinces: Galatia, Macedonia, Achaia and Asia. Prior to AD 47 there were no churches in these provinces, but by AD 57 Paul could speak of his work there as being completed according to Romans 15:19-20.

Apostles today may have gained a greater number of converts than Paul but, unfortunately, few have established growing churches like Paul did. Many apostles and church planters have traveled from place to place without any biblical plan or strategy. For the most part, modern day apostles have neither understood nor practiced Paul's method of church planting and establishing.

But some might say, "Things were different in Paul's day." Then one must ask the question, "Did Paul's situation contribute to his success?" Objectively, one must admit that Paul's converts were born and raised in similar social environments as we see in the world today. In Paul's day, human sacrifice was common and belief in witchcraft and demons was universal. It was the immutable Spirit of Christ that enabled the apostles to banish these demons from hearts. Deliverance came not by denial, but by conquest through preaching the supremacy of Christ in the power of the Holy Spirit! So, it is impossible to argue objectively that Paul's environment had any advantage over our world today; if anything, it was a disadvantage based on our methodology today.

As an introduction to Paul's church planting strategy, let us briefly observe four key elements of his strategy as it relates with today's church planting methodology:

Evangelizing

Paul's evangelizing consisted of preaching a pure gospel, Christ and Him crucified—the power of the Gospel unto salvation to all who believe. Paul's supreme subject was the Cross along with repentance and faith alone, not philosophy or psychology or some program trying to be relevant or tolerant. There was always an air of expectation pervading his preaching. His message stood alone. If people rejected him, he shook the dust off his feet and moved on to find more receptive hearts where God was at work. If we continue to preach the gospel where God is not at work, we degrade it to the level of merely educating people's intellect.

Another aspect of Paul's evangelizing was not to preach the gospel to every person in a particular area by himself. Today we send out individuals and teams that try to personally reach as many individuals in an area as possible by sharing the gospel. But by neglecting to use Paul's strategy of starting churches that are capable of spreading the gospel, we are severely limited in what a single person or team can do. Paul's goal was to establish reproducing churches that displayed the life of Christ in key strategic areas. Such areas exist today but are we utilizing them in our evangelistic strategies? It was from these churches located in key centers of intellectual and commercial activity that the gospel would spread in every direction.

Establishing

The second element of Paul's strategy was establishing. Paul established indigenous churches that were self-sustaining and could stand on their own. Instead of looking for support, these churches learned to depend on God and to not only share generously among themselves but with other churches. Paul's example to support himself by his own hands was one of the reasons these churches quickly learned to become self-sustaining. Paul was very careful to avoid any appearance of financial profiting or having financial motives from his ministry.

Today, many of our churches and mission organizations have become financial institutions rather than the living Body of Christ. We commonly hear that organizations are unable to plant churches, to extend their missions, or to support their training institutions without financial assistance because they have learned to depend on money rather than the Lord. Money subsidies create religious establishments that subsequently produce dependent converts who learn only to rely upon money instead of the Lord and the Holy Spirit.

Traditionally, the idea has been that the stability of the church depends upon owning land, the erection of a building, or being financially secure. When we have secured a building or have adequate financial support, we tend to think a church or mission is firmly established and approved by God. But, in reality, buildings and money have absolutely no power to produce spiritual fruit and can actually hinder spiritual results.

Equipping

The third element of Paul's strategy was equipping. Normally Paul preached in a place for months and then left behind an indigenous church capable of growth, expansion and producing elders for equipping the saints. This process included grave risks, but Paul had such faith in Christ and the Holy Spirit that he did not shrink from the risks. Many times Paul left his fledgling churches and elders with a simple system of gospel teaching, oversight or shepherding criteria and two sacraments with no fixed standard for meetings or gatherings.

Paul taught the common people, many who were unable to read, by using the Old Testament and what the apostles had seen with their eyes and heard with their ears. The simplicity and brevity of his gospel teaching constituted its power. By his leaving, the church was forced to think, speak, and serve on its own, although they were not totally free from the need for guidance and growth. He left elders with basic character and spiritual qualifications, and instructions on teaching and practicing sound doctrine.

Frequently, churches today are overly dependent on the one person who started that church or the "one pastor" who serves there. Often converts remain reliant upon that one pastor or apostle and his successor for generations. When Paul left a church in a timely manner, it gave the church leaders the opportunity to step into their proper roles and responsibilities, forcing them to realize that they could not depend upon the Apostle Paul.

Today, we are not training churches to use the gifts the Holy Spirit has given them. We overemphasize intellectual qualifications of leaders by relying heavily on artificial standards of formal education. Many times these worldly standards can even become a necessary requirement for ministry and leadership.

The new church should depend upon its own resources and more importantly, upon God. If any missionary today established a church like Paul, he might be told that his methods were hopeless and reckless. Yet the facts remain clear, Paul was the most successful founder of churches that this world has ever known.

Expanding

Finally, Paul's expanding strategy came as a result of the leadership of the Holy Spirit. It is interesting to observe that Paul's new converts naturally or maybe we should say, "supernaturally," became evangelists. Paul did not exhort people to become evangelists. Why? Because he knew when a person received the Spirit, they would begin to seek to bring others to the saving knowledge of Jesus as seen in Acts. This is not surprising since the Spirit that they and we receive is the missionary Spirit—the Spirit of Jesus who came into the world to redeem lost souls to the Father. We will learn from Acts how the churches were strengthened in faith and increased in number in Galatia, and how the Word of God spread to Macedonia and Achaia from Thessalonica, and how the gospel spread throughout neighboring countries from Ephesus.

Paul led them to the Spirit of Christ, whom they willingly submitted to. He set for them an example that was in accord with the mind of Christ. Paul was persuaded that the indwelling Spirit of

Christ in His power and passion would enable the church to expand. When the foundation of the church is not properly laid, I believe that the evangelistic Spirit is quenched resulting in a stagnant church. This is yet another compelling reason to use Paul's proven model and method of training; we are told to "follow Paul as he followed Christ".

Today's churches, for the most part, are stagnant and weak in comparison to the early church in Acts. Below are three disquieting symptoms we see in many of today's churches and missions. First we will observe these symptoms and then we will discuss each one so we can find solutions to these problems.

1. In today's church, there is little impact in its community and beyond. Most churches are not multiplying, disciples are not increasing and the Word of the Lord is not spreading like it did in the early church. Look at the map below and observe the dates attached to the geographical progress of the spread of the gospel.

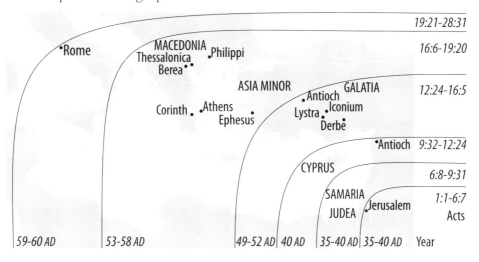

2. We have not succeeded in planting truly indigenous churches. In most countries outside of the West, the Christian faith is still considered a foreign religion. The diagram below helps explain this problem. For instance, in the early Jewish Church the Jews wanted the Gentiles to become Jewish in order to enter the kingdom and in today's western church, the West has sincerely and maybe unconsciously enticed other faiths to become western in order to enter the kingdom.

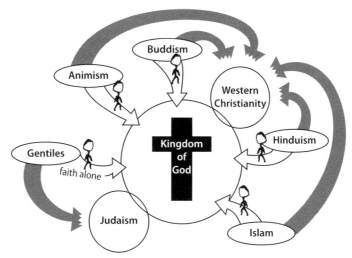

Explanation: In the early church Paul strongly opposed Gentiles becoming Jewish in order to enter the kingdom. Anything that added or took away from the gospel of grace was a false faith. Paul taught that it was "faith alone" in Christ which enabled a person to enter the kingdom. Paul's strong stand on grace moved the gospel from a Jewish context to a Gentile context in only twenty to thirty years. Today, the gospel has been in some countries for hundreds of years and is still not indigenous.

Therefore, there was a rapid expansion of the gospel from Jewish Jerusalem to the Gentile world. Modern day missions have unintentionally and sincerely told or have given the impression that new believers should become western in order to enter the church. Although God has used and continues to use modern day missions, no doubt our western methods have greatly hindered the expansion of the indigenous church, particularly among the third world people groups.

3. Most missions and churches in the third world are *not* self-sustaining. Most do not meet their own needs and continue to appeal for more money and resources. There is an unrealistic and unbiblical fear that without foreign support their church or mission will surely cease to exist. The diagram below uses the US and Asia as an example picturing this dependency on money.

Money stops = Ministry stops

As you can see, when a ministry, mission or church is built or connected with money, then its lifeblood can become money; therefore, when the money stops, the ministry stops. Money can become a substitute for the Holy Spirit and cause the mighty weapons of God to become power-less. When the church is connected to the Holy Spirit it is unstoppable and is a powerful force that the gates of hell cannot stop. Note: One of the purposes of this manual is to return to the way of Christ and the apostles so that the church today can be liberated from this type of dependency and become an unstoppable force in the world today.

A Return to the Scriptures

Project A
Contrasting the Early Church with Today's Church

Discuss together and answer the following questions. Don't be afraid to share your critical thoughts and concerns.

Why are most churches today not making the kind of progress that the early church did in spreading the Word and turning their communities and world upside down for Christ?

_____

_____

Would your church or ministry continue if the Holy Spirit was removed? What would change?

_____

_____

Why have we not been more successful in planting indigenous churches and ministries in the world today like the early Jewish Church did in the Gentile world?

_____

_____

Why are most of today's churches, ministries and missions still not self-sustaining like the churches that Paul established?

_____

_____

*God is moving today like **never** before in all of church history. What a great time to be alive! Today there are great "church planting movements" around the world and God is inviting you to join these movements, but first let us define a "church planting movement":*

> A church planting movement is an accelerated multiplication of indigenous disciples and churches planting churches. This movement flows through families and people groups, and is normally beyond the influence of those who introduced the gospel to them. Not only is the early church a historical example of this type of movement but China provides us with a modern day example. Several hundred years ago, Hudson Taylor (1832–1905), a missionary to China, introduced the gospel to the Chinese and today there is an extraordinary rapid church planting movement of God in China without significant Western involvement. Now let's look at the Bible concerning Church and Kingdom growth.

First of all, it is obvious from Jesus' teachings concerning His Kingdom that He expected dramatic and extraordinary growth. One of the many illustrations of this is the parable of the mustard seed in Matthew 13:31-32. The mustard seed is one of the smallest of seeds and when planted grows larger than all the other garden plants which have larger seeds. The end result of the tiny mustard seed is an enormous tree.

Secondly, Christ seemed to indicate that the gospel seed was to be implanted into other cultures indigenously as previously discussed. A brother in Burma told me that we planted the whole flower pot rather than the seed. Matthew 13:33 uses a "word picture" by comparing the gospel to being planted into a culture as yeast is to being mixed into a large amount of dough. The whole batch of dough is impacted from within by the yeast. We already discussed an illustration recorded in Acts, of cross-cultural evangelism when the Jewish church morphed into a Gentile church within twenty to thirty years. Yet today, after hundreds of years, Christianity still remains largely a foreign or Western religion, particularly in the 10/40 Window (to be discussed later in this manual) where most of the unreached people groups are located. When Christianity is perceived as a foreign faith or religion then this expected rapid spread of the gospel is dramatically hindered. So, what can we do? We can do things which, I believe, will "inhibit" the movement of God and there are things we can do or not do that "accelerate" the movement of God. We will call these "inhibitors" and "accelerators", respectively.

Accelerators are church planting actions or the absence of actions that may not be measurable and may take longer to see fruit but, ultimately, result in strong churches being established with lasting kingdom results. Note: One of the purposes of this manual is to help accelerate and sustain church planting movements by using supra-cultural and timeless principles. This will be accomplished by building biblical tracks for these church-planting movements to run on while laying a biblical foundation for the movement to stand on.

Inhibitors are church planting actions or omissions of actions that may bring measurable short-term results, but are much more likely to inhibit the church from becoming fruitful movements of Christ with lasting results. An example of this can be found with the Hmong people group in Vietnam and in other people groups around the world. Case studies that support this can be found in David Garrison's book, *Church Planting Movements*. Below I have started a list of accelerators and inhibitors which may or may not be accurate within your culture but will give you something to think about as we bridge God's supra-cultural timeless principles into today's church (see bottom diagram on page 34).

Accelerators	Inhibitors
Communal Society	Individualistic Society
Family Conversion Patterns	Breakdown of Family Order
Churches Planting Churches	Individualistic Evangelism
Training "in" Ministry	Academic Training "for" Ministry
Cultivate and Empower Indigenous Leadership	Start with Foreign Leadership
Debt Free or Financial Independence	Debt and Financial Dependence
Christ, Head of the Church	Pastor, or Man as Head of Church
Multiple Leaders with Equality	Single Leader with Authoritative Style
Preserve Insider Identity	Establish a Foreign Identity
House Churches or Temporary Buildings	Permanent Buildings and Land
Persecution and Suffering	Ease, Pleasure, and Entertainment
Penetrate Existing Communities with Gospel	Extract Believers into New Communities
Contextualized Worship and Sacraments	Adopt Foreign Practices for Gatherings
Preserve Local Financial Independence	Accept Foreign Money and Dependence
Leaders Tent-making, or Working for Needs	Leaders Dependent on Financial Support
Authority and Sufficiency of God's Word	Bible Not Enough
Devotion to Prayer and Christ	Organizational and Business Practices
Godliness	Worldliness
Rapid Incorporation of New Believers	Rigid Requirements for Membership
High Cost of Following Christ	No Cost to Follow Christ
Bold, Spirit-filled, and Fearless Faith	Human Eloquence and Intellect
Releasing Disciples and Leaders	Retaining Disciples and Leaders

Fill in the blanks on the following page, Project B, with your own list of accelerators and inhibitors that are relevant to your own situation and culture. Discuss and challenge these accelerators and inhibitors. But remember, they can change from time to time, and culture to culture.

Project B
Identifying Accelerators and Inhibitors

Accelerators	Inhibitors
Grace and Love	*Legalism and Selfishness*

The Holy Spirit is moving today and extending to each of you a personal invitation to join Him at work and be a part of this awesome adventure!

Will you go? Yes _____ No _____ ?

What is the Purpose of *God's Plan for His Church*

The purpose of this manual is to set forth the methods and principles used by the early church that produced such amazing results in a brief time, and to bridge those principles to today's church so that we may see amazing results for our Father's glory among all the people groups of the world.

What do we want to accomplish by completing this manual?

1. Restore or renew our courage and confidence in the authority and sufficiency of Scripture and the Holy Spirit to plant and establish growing churches.

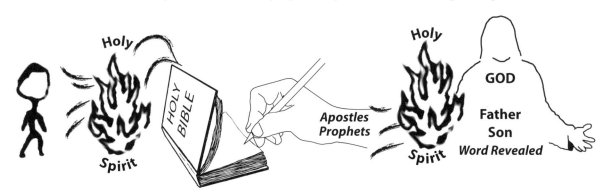

2. Paint a biblical vision of God's plan for His church today, not men's plan and not the western plan but God's Plan. The following diagram will serve as an illustration of God's plan detailed in this manual.

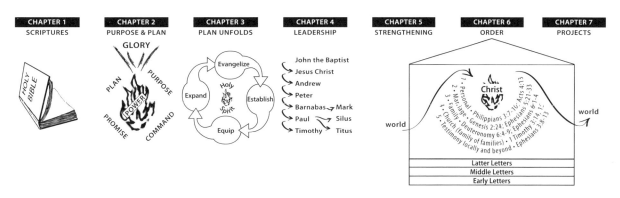

3. Start a journey of developing your own strategy of church planting and renewal. This strategy will be built on biblical, simple, practical, supra-cultural, and timeless principles and *not* a strategy that is dependent on man, buildings or money (See Project M, pages 231-234).

Review Chapter 1 before moving on to Chapter 2.

CHAPTER 1
SCRIPTURES

God makes it very clear in 2 Timothy 3:16-17 and 2 Peter 1:3-4 along with many other Scriptures that His Word is all we need. His Word *alone* provides the only textbook necessary for you to complete this manual. In Acts, God also makes it very clear that He has sent the gift of the Holy Spirit; it is no secret! In other words, we have everything we need to do what God has called us to do. This is our foundation that we will build upon. We will learn more concerning the sufficiency and authority of God's Word and the Holy Spirit in Lessons 47, page 188, and 50, page 195.

Chapter 2

OUR CHALLENGE

See God's Purpose and Plan

God's Ultimate Purpose is to Show Forth His Wisdom and Glory!

Scripture reveals God has a definite purpose and plan for His Church. The ultimate goal of His Church is not evangelizing, establishing, equipping or expanding but it is to make known His wisdom to the rulers and authorities in the heavenly places and for the earth to be filled with the knowledge of His glory. Therefore, we will see from Scripture that God's ultimate purpose and goal is accomplished through His Church by preaching the gospel and revealing His plan to all nations or people groups.

Project C
Revealing God's Purpose and Plan

What are two ways Paul was used to accomplish God's purpose and plan according to Ephesians 3:8-9?

1. First way was through _____ Ephesians 3:8*

2. Second way was through _____ Ephesians 3:9*

Why was Paul so devoted to planting and establishing churches according to Ephesians 3:10-11?*

_____

_____

_____

*Note: God's plan, and how Paul was used to fulfill that plan, will be developed more in Chapter 5 and 6.

God's Plan for His Church!

A. God's Plan

What is God's "plan" according to Matthew 16:18? _____

B. God's Promise

What is God's "promise" according to Mathew 16:18? _____

When will this promise be fulfilled according to Matthew 24:14? _____

How will this promise be fulfilled according to Matthew 24:14? _____

What is a nation? The word "nation" comes from the Greek word "ethnos" or "ethnic"; therefore, the literal meaning of nation is an ethnic group or a people group through which the gospel can flow without significant barriers of understanding like language, customs and family identities.

We will see on the next page that from Genesis to Revelation God has always desired redemption for all the people groups of the world. It is through these people groups that God will fill the earth with His Glory. Read the following verses and write what you learn about God's will for all the people groups of the world:

Genesis 12:1-3 _____

Psalms 67 _____

Habakkuk 1:5; 2:14 _____

Matthew 28:19-20 _____

Revelation 5:9; 14:6; 21:24; 22:1-5 _____

Most of the people groups who have not been reached with the gospel are located in what is called the 10/40 Window. See map below and identify the area you live in. Are you in the area God wants you to be?

The 10/40 Window comprises ⅓ of the world's land and ⅔ of the world's people. Ninety-five percent of these people have not even heard the gospel and eighty-five percent of them are among the poorest in the world. For more information see www.joshuaproject.net.

C. God's Command

What is God's "command" according to Matthew 28:19-20? _____
_____

What is God's "command" according to Mark 16:15? _____
_____

How is God's "command" to be carried out according to John 20:21? _____
_____

Where is God's "command" to be carried out according to Luke 24:46-47? _____
_____

D. God's Power

What is God's "power" according to Acts 1:8? _____

_____

When will his disciples receive this "power" according to Acts 1:8? _____

_____

What will his disciples become when they receive this "power" according to Acts 1:8? _____

_____

Where will his disciples be a "witness" according to Acts 1:8? _____

_____

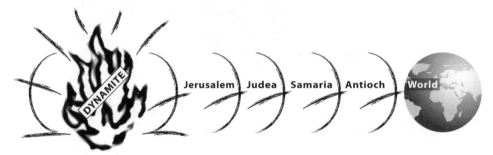

When was the promised Holy Spirit sent to His disciples according to Acts 2:1-4? _____

_____

If the Holy Spirit was sent at Pentecost, then why does today's church look and act more pre-Pentecostal (Before Pentecost) than post-Pentecostal (After Pentecost)?

_____

_____

A Chinese Christian leader, after visiting the USA was asked what impressed him most about the churches and ministries in the US. He thought and replied, "I am amazed what they can do without the Holy Spirit." What an indictment against the Western Church! Let us stop right here before proceeding any further and make sure we are not like the Laodicean Church who thought they were rich and had no need of the Holy Spirit, not realizing they were "wretched, pitiable, poor, blind, and naked". Turn now and read together Revelation 3:14-22. As you observe from Scripture, God provides a way back into the way of Christ and the apostles. Right now He is standing at the door of our hearts begging and knocking for us to open. If we will invite Him in, He will come in and take over our lives. Do you hear Him knocking today?

It has been said that we are as close to God as we want to be, and likewise, I believe our churches are as much like Acts as we sincerely desire them to be. Are you tired of the same old same old? Then turn back! Jesus says, "Be zealous and repent!" Otherwise this will be just another superficial, powerless and wasted study. Jesus said rivers of living water would flow out of us (John 7:38-39). The Holy Spirit is "able and desiring to do exceedingly abundantly more than we ask or think according to His power at work within us" (Ephesians 3:20). Please do not quench, resist or grieve the Holy Spirit. He is pleading and begging to take over our lives and ministries.

This is a new day; we cannot and will not go back. Forgetting those things which are behind, let us today repent and start anew and afresh to walk in the way of Christ and the Holy Spirit. (Note: More on the powerful work of the Holy Spirit will be developed in Acts and Lesson 50, page 195.)

Review Chapter 1 and 2 before moving on to Chapter 3.

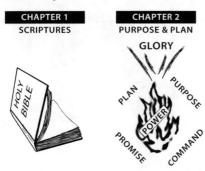

God's Word makes it very clear in John 5:17-19 and Acts 1:4-8, along with many other Scriptures, that you can do nothing of value without the Holy Spirit. God's Word and the Holy Spirit provide everything you need to complete this manual and fulfill God's call upon your life. The Word of God is your foundation and the Holy Spirit is your power. We will learn much more on the sufficiency of God's Word in Lesson 47 and the power of the Holy Spirit in Lesson 50.

Chapter 3

OUR CHALLENGE
Understand God's Plan

The Holy Spirit Comes and God's Plan for His Church Unfolds

We have learned that God has a plan to reveal His manifold wisdom to the rulers and authorities in heavenly places. God's purpose and plan is to be accomplished through His Church by preaching the gospel and revealing the mystery.

Now we embark on a journey like no other. We will take a close look at the historical writings in Acts that focus on the establishment and growth of the early church. The church was not only born, it gave birth to a powerful force that literally turned the world upside down in ways nobody would have imagined or thought possible. Truly this will be an unforgettable journey; therefore, fasten your seat belts and hold on as we join the movement of the Holy Spirit through Acts.

Through these lessons and projects, you will discern God's timeless and supra-cultural key principles in church establishing. It is important to recognize those principles that stay consistent throughout the book of Acts. You will compare and contrast the early church with today's church so you can discover what strengths and weaknesses are in today's church. In doing this, you will be able to see where changes need to be made and how to bring today's church more in line with the Scriptures. Then you will be equipped to start a new work or to renew an existing work. With that in mind let's dig into the historical record of this dynamic and exciting early church recorded for us in the book of Acts. To start with, let us get a picture of the book of Acts by looking at the map on the next page:

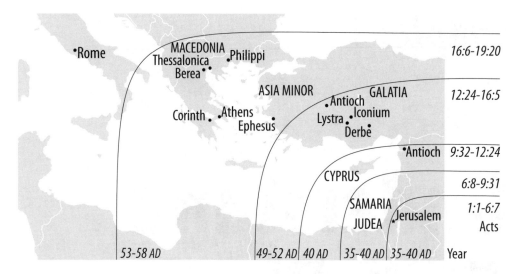

The following labels appear on the map:

• Rome

MACEDONIA
Thessalonica •Philippi
Berea •

ASIA MINOR

GALATIA
•Antioch
Corinth •Athens   Lystra •Iconium
      Ephesus •   Derbe •

                        •Antioch   *9:32-12:24*

CYPRUS   *6:8-9:31*

SAMARIA   *1:1-6:7*
JUDEA Jerusalem   Acts

16:6-19:20
12:24-16:5

53-58 AD   *49-52 AD* | *40 AD* | *35-40 AD* | *35-40 AD*   Year

Before we start our journey we need to consider how to connect what we learn in historical Acts, the "then" with the "now" regarding today's church. The bridge that connects Acts with today's church should be made of principles that will fit into any culture at any time. Let us observe the following chart that illustrates how we can connect or bridge the early church with today's church:

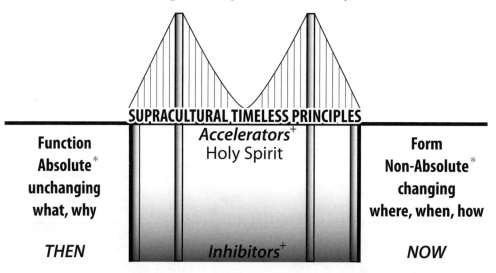

SUPRACULTURAL TIMELESS PRINCIPLES

Function Absolute* unchanging what, why	*Accelerators*+ Holy Spirit	Form Non-Absolute* changing where, when, how
THEN	*Inhibitors*+	*NOW*

With this objective in mind let us begin this incredible, exciting and challenging journey of the Holy Spirit working through His church.

*See Project D, pages 54-55.   +See Project B, pages 22-24.

Lesson 1
Expanding Churches: Jerusalem • Acts 1:1-6:7

This is the first of six divisions in the book of Acts. In this first division the Holy Spirit comes upon the disciples at Pentecost giving birth to the church. This ignites a fire beginning in Jerusalem and spreading to Judea, Samaria and to the ends of the earth. This division involves primarily Jews.

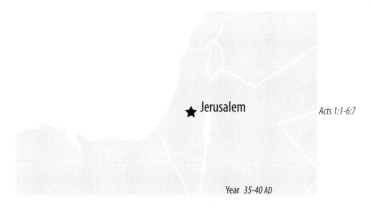

★ Jerusalem   *Acts 1:1-6:7*

Year 35-40 AD

Observation: Read and observe the following Scripture (Acts 1:1–6:7) and write down the keys that were useful in the expansion of the church from Jerusalem. *Note: As an example, the first blanks are filled in.*

Example: Acts 1:1-5 _Jesus gave commands through the Holy Spirit, chose Apostles, ordered them to wait for the Holy Spirit; John baptized with water, Jesus baptized with Holy Spirit._

Acts 1:6-11 _____

_____

Acts 1:12-14 _____

_____

Acts 1:15-26 _____

_____

Acts 2:1-13 _____

_____

Acts 2:14-41 _____

_____

Acts 2:42-47 _____

Acts 3:1-10 _____

_____

Acts 3:11-26 _____

_____

Acts 4:1-22 _____

_____

Acts 4:23-31 _____

_____

Acts 4:32-37 _____

_____

Acts 5:1-11 _____

_____

Acts 5:12-16 _____

_____

Acts 5:17-42 _____

_____

Acts 6:1-7 _____

_____

Respond: Based on the keys you recorded above, write in each column below a 2-3 word summary of those keys that every person, family and church could follow at any time, in any culture. Example given in first 3 rows of each column.	**Discussion:** In this column, contrast the key principles you recorded in the left column with your life, family and church experience today.
Commands Given by Holy Spirit 1:2	Given by man instead of Holy Spirit
Jesus chose Apostles 1:2	Many do not believe apostles are for today
Baptism of the Holy Spirit 1:5	We do the water but neglect the Spirit

Based on your discussion above, what are some changes you need to make in your life, family and church here and now? _____

_____

Application: How and when will you make these changes in your life, family and church?

_____

_____

_____

Lesson 2
Expanding Churches: Judea and Samaria • Acts 6:8-9:31

This is the second of six divisions in the book of Acts. The Holy Spirit having come upon the disciples in Jerusalem results in the persecution of the newly born church. The persecution scatters the church to Samaria. Now the Jewish church is becoming mixed with Gentiles.

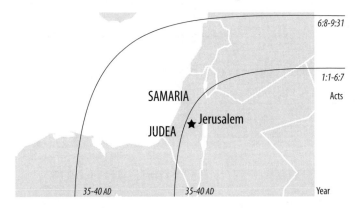

Observation: Read and observe the following Scripture (Acts 6:8–9:31) and write down all the keys that were useful in the expansion of the church into Judea and Samaria.

Example: Acts 6:8-15 <u>Stephen was full of grace and power doing great wonders and signs, speaking with wisdom and Spirit, He was falsely accused, His face was like the face of an angel.</u>

Acts 7:1-53 _____

_____

_____

Acts 7:54-60 _____

_____

Acts 8:1-8 _____

_____

_____

Acts 8:9-25 _____

_____

_____

Acts 8:26-40 _____

_____

_____

Acts 9:1-19 _____

_____

_____

Acts 9:20-25 _____

_____

_____

Acts 9:26-31 _____

_____

_____

Respond: Based on the keys you recorded above, write in each column below a 2-3 word summary of those keys that every person, family and church could follow at any time, in any culture. Example given in first 3 rows of each column.	**Discussion:** In this column, contrast the key principles you recorded in the left column with your life, family and church experience today.
Stephen was full of grace 6:8	Full of flesh and works, forget about grace
He did great wonders and signs 6:8	Do not see wonders and signs
He spoke with wisdom and the Spirit 6:10	Speak with man's wisdom and intellect

Based on your discussion above, what are some changes you need to make in your life, family and church here and now? _____

_____

_____

Application: How and when will you make these changes in your life, family and church.

_____

_____

_____

Lesson 3
Expanding Churches: Antioch • Acts 9:32-12:24

This is the third of six divisions in the book of Acts. Persecution leads the church to expand to Antioch. The key leadership and work of the Holy Spirit shifts from Peter and the Jews to Paul and the Gentiles. The Word continues to spread and multiply.

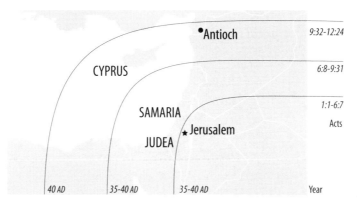

Observation: Read and observe the following Scripture (Acts 9:32–12:24) and write down all the keys that were useful in the expansion of the church into Antioch.

Example: Acts 9:32-35 *Peter travels among the people, Jesus heals Aeneas through Peter and people turned to Lord.*

Acts 9:36-43 _____

_____

_____

Acts 10:1-8 _____

_____

_____

Acts 10:9-33 _____

_____

_____

Acts 10:34-43 _____

_____

_____

Acts 10:44-48 _____

_____

_____

Acts 11:1-18 _____

_____

_____

Acts 11:19-30 _____

_____

_____

Acts 12:1-5 _____

_____

Acts 12:6-19 _____

_____

_____

Acts 12:20-24 _____

_____

_____

Respond: Based on the keys you recorded above, write in each column below a 2-3 word summary of those keys that every person, family and church could follow at any time, in any culture. Example given in first 3 rows of each column.	**Discussion:** In this column, contrast the key principles you recorded in the left column with your life, family and church experience today.
Peter traveled here and there 9:32	Stay in one location or building
Jesus heals Aeneas through Peter 9:34	It is all about medicine and doctors today
People turn to the Lord 9:35	People turn to themselves and religion

Based on your discussion above, what are some changes you need to make in your life, family and church here and now? _____

_____

_____

Application: How and when will you make these changes in your life, family and church?

_____

_____

_____

Lesson 4
Expanding Churches: Asia Minor •
Acts 12:25–16:5

Now we see the establishment of the Antioch church which becomes a launching pad for the gospel to the ends of the earth. The Holy Spirit sends out their two key men, Paul and Barnabas to Asia Minor. The church is strengthened in faith and increases in numbers daily.

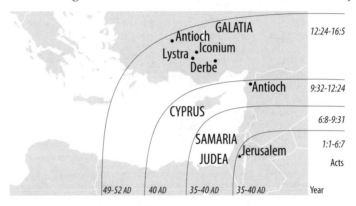

Observation: Read and observe the following Scripture (Acts 12:25–16:5) and write down all the keys that were useful in the expansion of the church into Asia Minor.

Example: Acts 12:25–13:3 <u>Added Mark</u> to their team, they were <u>fasting and worshiping</u> the Lord, the <u>Holy Spirit set apart</u> Paul and Barnabas for service, laid hands on and <u>sent them.</u>

Acts 13:4-12 _____

_____

_____

Acts 13:13-52 _____

_____

_____

Acts 14:1-7 _____

_____

Acts 14:8-18 _____

_____

_____

Acts 14:19-23 _____

_____

_____

Acts 14:24-28 _____

_____

_____

Acts 15:1-21 _____

_____

_____

Acts 15:22-35 _____

_____

_____

Acts 15:36-41 _____

_____

_____

Acts 16:1-5 _____

_____

_____

Respond: Based on the keys you recorded above, write in each column below a 2-3 word summary of those keys that every person, family and church could follow at any time, in any culture. Example given in first 3 rows of each column.	**Discussion:** In this column, contrast the key principles you recorded in the left column with your life, family and church experience today.
They worshiped the Lord and fasted 13:2	No fasting today, use human wisdom
Holy Spirit set apart Paul and Barnabas 13:2	Man sets people apart for service
Laid hands on them and sent them off 13:3	Don't send very many people today

Based on your discussion above, what are some changes you need to make in your life, family and church here and now? _____

_____

_____

Application: How and when will you make these changes in your life, family and church?

_____

_____

_____

Lesson 5
Expanding Churches: Aegean Area •
Acts 16:6–19:20

Now we see the establishment of the church on the Aegean shores. The Holy Spirit is clearly directing the apostles to preach the gospel, to strengthen the disciples and appoint elders in every church. And the Word of God continues to increase and prevail mightily.

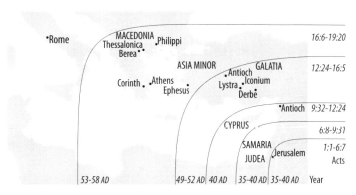

Observation: Read and observe the following Scripture (Acts 16:6–19:20) and write down all the keys that were useful in the expansion of the church into the Aegean area.

Example: Acts 16:6-10 <u>They were forbidden to speak the word by the Holy Spirit, a vision appeared to Paul, Paul immediately obeyed</u> the vision, they were <u>called to preach the gospel.</u>

Acts 16:11-15 _____

_____

Acts 16:16-24 _____

_____

Acts 16:25-40 _____

_____

Acts 17:1-9 _____

_____

Acts 17:10-15 _____

_____

_____

Acts 17:16-21 _____

_____

Acts 17:22-34 _____

_____

_____

Acts 18:1-17 _____

_____

_____

Acts 18:18-23 _____

_____

_____

Acts 18:24-28 _____

_____

Acts 19:1-10 _____

_____

Acts 19:11-20 _____

_____

Respond: Based on the keys you recorded above, write in each column below a 2-3 word summary of those keys that every person, family and church could follow at any time, in any culture. Example given in first 3 rows of each column.	**Discussion:** In this column, contrast the key principles you recorded in the left column with your life, family and church experience today.
Holy Spirit forbids them to speak 16:6	We do not listen and obey the Holy Spirit
A vision appeared to Paul at night 16:9	No visions today, wonder why?
They immediately obeyed the Holy Spirit 16:10	No immediate obedience today

Based on your discussion above, what are some changes you need to make in your life, family and church here and now? _____

_____

_____

Application: How and when will you make these changes in your life, family and church?

_____

_____

_____

Lesson 6
Expanding Churches: Roman Empire • Acts 19:21-28:31

Paul plans to visit Rome but how he gets there is an unforeseen journey. After leaving the elders in Ephesus, Paul goes to Jerusalem where, after his arrest, he appeals to Caesar. This takes him to Rome where he preaches the Gospel with all boldness and without hindrance.

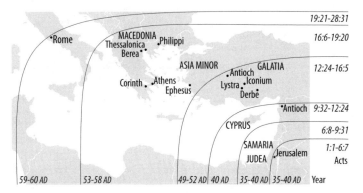

Observation: Read and observe the following Scripture (Acts 19:21–28:31) and write down all the keys that were useful in the expansion of the church into the Roman Empire.

Example: Acts 19:21-40 <u>The Holy Spirit directs</u> Paul's travels, <u>sends out his helpers</u>, Paul persuades <u>people to turn away from false gods</u> which leads to a loss of income and confusion.

Acts 20:1-6 _____

_____

_____

Acts 20:7-16 _____

_____

_____

Acts 20:17-38 _____

_____

_____

Acts 21:1-16 _____

_____

_____

Acts 21:17-26 _____
_____
_____

Acts 21:27-36 _____
_____
_____

Acts 21:37–22:21 _____
_____
_____

Acts 22:22-29 _____
_____
_____

Acts 22:30–23:11 _____
_____
_____

Acts 23:12-22 _____
_____
_____

Acts 23:23-35 _____
_____
_____

Acts 24:1-21 _____
_____
_____

Acts 24:22-27 _____
_____

Acts 25:1-12 _____
_____

Acts 25:13-27 _____
_____
_____

Acts 26:1-11 _____

_____

_____

Acts 26:12-32 _____

_____

Acts 27:1-12 _____

_____

Acts 27:13-38 _____

_____

Acts 27:39-44 _____

_____

Acts 28:1-10 _____

_____

Acts 28:11-16 _____

_____

Acts 28:17-31 _____

_____

Respond: Based on the keys you recorded above, write in each column below a 2-3 word summary of those keys that every person, family and church could follow at any time, in any culture. Example given in first 3 rows of each column.	**Discussion:** In this column, contrast the key principles you recorded in the left column with your life, family and church experience today.
Holy Spirit directs Paul's travels 19:21	Man's wisdom and studies direct our travels
Paul sends helpers to other cities 19:22	One man show and do not send out
People turn away from their gods 19:26	No turning today, can keep gods and be okay

Based on your discussion above, what are some changes you need to make in your life, family and church here and now? _____

_____

_____

Application: How and when will you make these changes in your life, family and church?

_____

_____

_____

Project D
Discerning Absolutes from Non-Absolutes

In Lesson 7 we will summarize the book of Acts by going back and selecting four keys from each of the six lessons that you put in your Respond columns. We want to bridge the "then" with the "now" by developing a list of consistent supra-cultural and timeless principles used throughout the book of Acts with today's church here and now (see bottom diagram on page 34).

Before we get started with Lesson 7, let us explain what supra-cultural and timeless principles are. These principles can be defined as absolute principles or functions that never change with culture or time. The opposite of these absolutes are non-absolutes which are forms that can change with culture and time. It is with these absolute principles that we want to bridge the "then" in Acts with the "now," today's church.

The charts and diagrams below will help us determine the difference between absolutes and non-absolutes. We can also see how people naturally fixate on forms, finding it very difficult to change without a crisis. When we are locked into a form and refuse to change, it can cause the function to die, having a form without the power. Working and discussing these charts together will help you glean those absolutes from Scripture and bridge today's church with those powerful biblical principles in Acts.

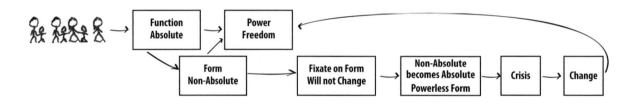

Read Hebrews 10:24-25 and contrast absolutes with non-absolutes. For example, is "meeting together" an absolute or non-absolute? Yes, it is an absolute, but where we meet and when we meet, is a non-absolute. Let me ask you; is a church building an absolute or non-absolute? Is "encouraging one another" absolute or non-absolute? Place these items in the appropriate box below and discuss. You can do this with the Sabbath, evangelism, prayer, baptism, pulpit, tracts, Bible versions, hymns, music, communion, serving and loving one another etc. List as many absolute functions and non-absolute forms as you can in the columns below and discuss together. Be careful that non-absolutes (Functions) do not become absolutes (Forms) because you will lose your freedom, joy, and power.

Absolutes	Non-Absolutes
Meeting together	Meeting in church building on Sunday morning

When you have finished discussing and everyone has a fairly clear understanding of these supra-cultural timeless absolutes (Functions) and non-absolutes (Forms) then move on to Lesson 7.

Lesson 7
Expanding Churches: Jerusalem to Ends of the Earth • Acts

You have just embarked on an incredible journey like no other in all of history. Obviously what made the difference in this journey was the coming and empowering of the Holy Spirit. Without Him there would be no book of Acts, but by Him the church was born and it impacted the world from Jerusalem to the ends of the earth.

Observation: Summarize the book of Acts by going back and selecting four keys from each of the six lessons that you put in your Respond columns. Be sure that each key you select is consistent throughout the book of Acts and that each key will fit into any culture (supra-cultural) at any time (timeless).

Example: Acts 1:1-6:7   They were devoted to prayer 1:14, they were filled with the Holy Spirit 2:4–8, they repented 2:38, they were devoted to the apostles teaching, breaking of bread, and fellowship 2:42, they obeyed the Holy Spirit 5:32

Acts 6:8–9:31 _____

Acts 9:32–12:24 _____

Acts 12:25–16:5 _____

Acts 16:6–19:20 _____

_____

_____

_____

_____

Acts 19:21–28:31 _____

_____

_____

_____

_____

Discussion: Contrast these principles with your life, family and church experience today.

_____

_____

_____

_____

What changes do you need to make in your life, family and church here and now? _____

_____

_____

_____

_____

Application: How and when will you make these changes in your life, family and church?

_____

_____

_____

_____

Lesson 8
Paul's Missionary Strategy

Paul was a master church builder who founded thriving and growing churches in main centers of population. These churches had the responsibility of establishing other churches in their surrounding areas and beyond. Paul overcame three hindrances that we previously discussed in church expansion today; he established indigenous and self-sustaining churches that were capable of multiplying by themselves.

Observation: Read and observe the following verses and write down the key elements or principles of Paul's missionary strategy from the Word of God.

Example: Ephesians 3:8 _Preach the unsearchable riches of Christ._

Ephesians 3:9 _____

Ephesians 3:10 _____

Matthew 16:18 _____

Matthew 28:19-20 _____

Acts 1:8 _____

Acts 2:1-4 _____

Acts 2:42-47 _____

Acts 11:22-26 _____

Acts 13:1-4 _____

_____

Acts 14:7 _____

_____

Acts 14:21 _____

_____

Acts 14:22 _____

_____

Acts 14:23 _____

_____

Acts 14:26-27 _____

_____

Acts 20:17-38 _____

_____

Romans 15:19-20 _____

_____

Respond: Based on these verses, write a brief summary of the key elements or functions of Paul's missionary strategy that you observed from God's Word that every person, family and church could follow at any time, in any culture. (Absolutes)

_____

_____

Discussion: Contrast these principles with what your life, family and church experience today.

_____

_____

What changes do you need to make in your life, family and church here and now? _____

_____

_____

Application: How and when will you make these changes in your life, family and church?

_____

_____

Our Example: The Antioch Church

To form a biblical picture of an established church you can examine the church as it expanded to Antioch. It developed through these four basic stages:

1. **Building** a community base (Jerusalem) Acts 2:38-47

2. **Overseeing** expansion of the gospel from Jews to the Gentiles (Jerusalem to Antioch) Acts 3–12

3. **Establishing** churches (Antioch) Acts 11:19-26

4. **Sending** out proven leaders (Antioch to the World) Acts 13:1-3

Paul's plan had four basic stages: Acts 11:19–14:26

1. **Evangelizing**—getting the message to strategic cities, Romans 15:14-21
   Phase One: Gathering a beachhead of disciples, Acts 11:19-21
   Phase Two: Expose the life of Christ to the community, Acts 11:26

2. **Establishing**—by forming these communities of disciples into churches, Acts 14:22

3. **Equipping**—by appointing elders to equip the disciples, Acts 14:23

4. **Expanding**—by listening to the Holy Spirit in the sending process (Acts 13:1-3) by identifying and equipping emerging leaders called apostles or church planters (Acts 16:1-5) by passing the care of the church on to elders (Acts 20:17-28) and by leaving them instructions for establishing and training faithful men (1 and 2 Timothy; Titus).

Now you can start to visualize church development in four basic stages and you can see how they build upon one another:

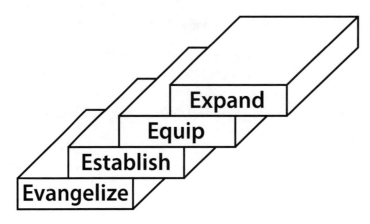

Lesson 9
Antioch Church Model

After observing so much Scripture, we begin to see a pattern emerging. The following verses will allow you to visualize an established church which naturally flows from four basic stages of development. You will learn how they build upon one another in a predictable cycle.

Observation: Read and observe the following verses and write down the biblical support for the four key elements or principles of *Paul's Missionary Strategy* from the Word of God.

Expanding

Example: Matthew 28:19a *Jesus said to go and make disciples of all nations, baptizing, teaching*
_____

Acts 11:22-24a _____
_____
_____

Acts 13:1-4 _____
_____
_____

Acts 16:1-3 _____
_____
_____

Romans 15:19-20 _____
_____
_____

Evangelizing

Matthew 28:19 _____
_____
_____

Acts 11:19-21 _____

_____

_____

Acts 13:32 _____

_____

_____

Acts 13:47-49 _____

_____

_____

Acts 14:5-7 _____

_____

_____

Establishing

Matthew 28:20 _____

_____

_____

Acts 11:25-26 _____

_____

_____

Acts 14:23 _____

_____

_____

Acts 16:4-5 _____

_____

_____

Acts 18:23 _____

_____

_____

Equipping

Acts 14:23 _____

_____

_____

Acts 20:17-38 _____

_____

_____

Ephesians 4:11-14 _____

_____

_____

Titus 1:5-9 _____

_____

_____

1 Peter 5:1-5 _____

_____

_____

Respond: Based on these verses, write a brief summary of each of the four key elements or functions of Paul's missionary strategy that you observed from God's Word that every person, family and church could follow at any time, in any culture. (Absolutes)

Expanding _____

_____

Evangelizing _____

_____

Establishing _____

_____

Equipping _____

_____

Discussion: Contrast these four flowing principles with what your life, family and church experience today. _____

_____

_____

_____

What changes do you need to make in your life, family and church here and now? _____

_____

_____

_____

Application: How and when will you make these changes in your life, family and church?

_____

_____

_____

God's Pattern Revealed

After observing Scripture, do you see a pattern emerging?

As with many things, there is a predictable cycle that shows how a healthy church develops:

Evangelize: This is the process used to get the message to the people most effectively.

Establish: This is the process that brings the new believers to a sure or firm foundation in the faith and the gospel of grace.

Equip: This is the process of appointing elders who spiritually feed and lead and oversee the flock, the church.

Expand: The natural development of an established church, which reaches out further into the community with the gospel. This growth is measured by the church's ability to *release, not retain,* disciples. This cycle is seen over and over in Paul's writings.

These processes flow in succession like this:

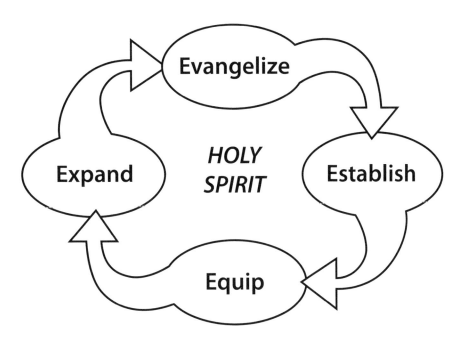

Book of Acts Conclusion

(A Condensed Definition of Church Planting and Renewal)

The main purpose of church planting and renewal is to plant new churches where none exist and to strengthen existing churches where they do exist.

God's Plan for His Church Unfolds

Project E
Developing Your Own Strategy

We have learned so much from the Scriptures. Now it is time to condense it down to the key principles and discover how God will use you in your location to start a new church or to renew an existing church. This project will get you started on the completion of your final project in Part 6. (You can write your answer or answer with a chart or diagram.)

1. Develop a brief and simple strategy for starting a new church where none exists that can be carried out in any culture and any time.

   _____

   _____

2. Develop a strategy for renewing or establishing an existing church that can be carried out in any culture and anytime.

   _____

   _____

3. Personalize this new and/or renewal strategy by bridging what you have learned from Acts with your "today's" church:

   _____

   _____

4. Make a list of prayer requests concerning your role in starting a new church or renewing a church locally and beyond.

   _____

   _____

Begin praying now, both individually and corporately!

Review Chapter 1, 2 and 3 before going on to Chapter 4.

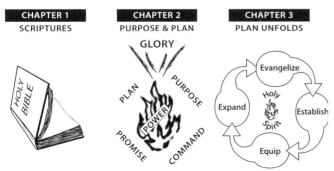

Chapter 4

OUR CHALLENGE

Develop Faithful Leaders in the Church

Biblical Principles of Leadership Development

Obviously, some leaders view the western model of training disciples and leaders superior to how Jesus and the early church trained disciples, otherwise, there would be a desire to return to the way of Christ and the apostles. Where did today's training methods originate? Are they biblical? Are they better? When you look at the expansion of the early church, the life of the early disciples and apostles, and the impact they had on their world, you must conclude we are not doing a better job of training today. Something is missing. Those early disciples, full of the Holy Spirit, left all and gave all for their Savior turning their world upside down for Christ. To understand the leadership deficiency in the church today, let's look at the following chart:

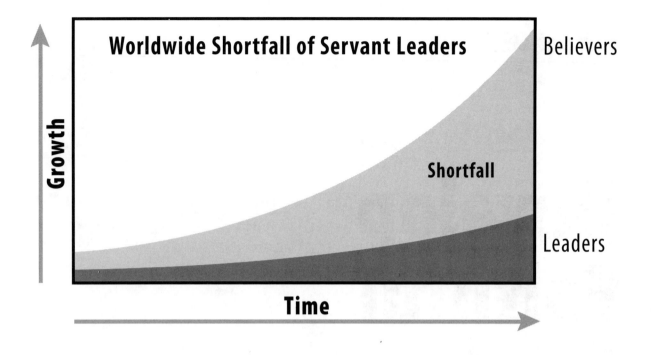

Worldwide Shortfall of Servant Leaders

Growth

Believers

Shortfall

Leaders

Time

Discussion Questions: Why does the growth of leadership not keep pace with the church growth? _____

_____

_____

_____

How can we illuminate or reduce this shortfall of leadership in the world today?

_____

_____

_____

_____

Now on the next page, let's talk about four of today's failings of church leadership that might have contributed to the church becoming stagnant and weak in its impact and expansion.

Project F
Contrasting Today's Leadership Training with the Early Church

1. How has the church's failure to recognize and practice the sufficiency and authority of Scripture in training leaders contributed to this weakness in today's church? (2 Timothy 3:16-17)

   _____

   _____

2. How has the church by not emphasizing the family concept and proper biblical roles, contributed to this weakness in today's church?

   _____

   _____

3. Why is positional and institutional leadership more acceptable today than Spirit filled servant leadership?

   _____

4. Was Jesus and Paul's strategy to retain or release disciples? _____

   Why do you think that churches today desire more to retain disciples and leaders than to release disciples and leaders? _____

   _____

   _____

Note: A word of caution—when you do things biblically, especially servant leadership and releasing, you must measure biblically or otherwise, you will be discouraged and rejected by today's church.

In the early church leadership training and development was key to this tremendous progress and impact. Therefore, let us travel back and start with John the Baptist who paved the way for Jesus. He sets forth a very important key ingredient that undergirds the type of leadership expressed in the early church, which we desperately need in today's church. John's key leadership principle was the supra-cultural and timeless principle of increasing Jesus and decreasing himself (John 3:30).

John the Baptist paved the way for Jesus. After that, who was the first disciple that Jesus called? _____ And, who did Andrew call? _____ And so, the "twelve disciples" were chosen.

According to tradition, Peter, a leader in the early Jerusalem Church, was trained and mentored by Jesus. According to tradition, Peter then trained and mentored Barnabas in the context of the early church in Jerusalem. So when the early church looked for a key man with godly character to send to Antioch, they sent Barnabas. It is through Barnabas that the early church expands to Antioch where a church is established by Barnabas, who is joined by the Apostle Paul. The Antioch Church becomes a launching pad to take the gospel to the world.

Now starting with Barnabas, we will follow the key thread of leadership that connected or held together the expansion of the early church from Jerusalem to the world (see chart below). We will see how leaders, church planters and elders emerged from the church family of God for the next generation.

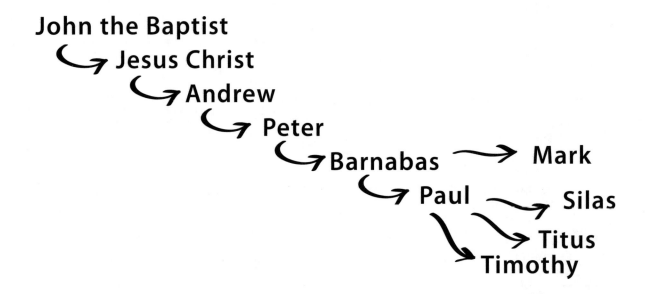

Now let's return to the Scriptures in Lessons 10-17 and see how leaders emerged and were sent out in the early church. We will see how apostles developed elders and trained other apostles for the next generation. These leaders were unlikely men and women who were tested and proven by God in the context of the church family.

Lesson 10
Apostles Emerged in the Early Church •
Acts 4:36–11:36

Instructions: Answer the questions below in the blanks based on the Bible verses beside the questions.

Barnabas' character was proven (Acts 4:36-37; 9:26-27)

1. What can you learn from Barnabas' name? (4:36)

_____

_____

2. What makes you think Barnabas was devoted to the Lord? (4:37) _____

_____

3. What indicates Barnabas was a man under authority? (4:37b) _____

_____

4. Why would Barnabas make a good partner in the ministry? (9:26-27) _____

_____

Barnabas was sent out by the Jerusalem Church (Acts 11:19-23)

5. Why was Barnabas sent to Antioch? (11:19-23) _____

6. What did Barnabas do when he arrived at Antioch? (11:23b) _____

_____

Barnabas' qualifications for church planting (Acts 11:24-26)

7. What kind of man was Barnabas? (11:24) _____

_____

8. Barnabas was a man full of the Holy Spirit. Why is this an important qualification? (11:24)

_____

9. Why is the qualification of being filled with the Holy Spirit often neglected today? _____

_____

10. Barnabas was a man full of faith. What does being full of faith mean? (11:24) _____

_____

11. Who did Barnabas get to help him? Why? (11:25, 26) _____

_____

12. How long did Barnabas and Paul stay in Antioch? What did they do while there? (11:26)

_____

_____

13. What were the disciples first called in Antioch? (11:26b) Why? _____

_____

Discussion: What seems to be the most important aspect of Barnabas' life that made him qualified to be sent out by the Jerusalem Church? _____

_____

_____

_____

Why is education often more important than character and being filled with the Holy Spirit and faith? _____

_____

_____

_____

_____

Lesson 11
Apostles Sent out by the Early Church •
Acts 13:1–14:27

Apostles were developed to be sent out (Acts 13:1-4).

1. Who were the leaders, prophets and teachers in the Antioch Church? (13:1) _____

_____

2. Where do you think these leaders were trained? (13:1) _____

_____

3. Who do you think were the two key leaders in this group of men? (13:1-2) _____

_____

4. What were they doing when the Holy Spirit spoke to them? (13:2) _____

_____

5. Who sent Barnabas and Paul out? (13:2-4) _____

_____

6. Who else was involved in this sending process? (13:1-4) _____

_____

7. Describe the total picture of this sending process. (13:1-4) _____

_____

Apostles had a strategy (Acts 14:21-27)

8. What was the first thing these apostles did when they arrived at a city? (14:6; 21a) _____

_____

9. What was the result of the apostles' preaching the gospel? (14:21b) _____

_____

10. Why did the apostles return to Lystra, Iconium and Antioch? (14:22) _____

_____

11. Who did the apostles appoint in every church? (14:23) _____

_____

12. How did they appoint them? (14:23) _____

_____

13. Who did the apostles commit them to? (14:23b) _____

_____

14. Where did the apostles return to when they completed their missionary trip? Why? (14:26-27)

_____

_____

_____

Discussion: Who sent out Paul and Barnabas? _____

What were they doing when the Holy Spirit sent them out? _____

_____

_____

_____

Why is the Holy Spirit often neglected in the sending process in today's church? _____

_____

_____

_____

_____

God's Plan for Strong Leaders in the Church

Lesson 12
Apostles Developed Elders in the Early Church • Acts 20:17-38

Paul's training strategy for elders (Acts 20:17-26)

1. Where did Paul live in Ephesus? (20:18) _____

2. How did Paul serve the Ephesians? (20:19) _____
_____

3. What did Paul preach to them? (20:20) _____
_____

4. Where did Paul teach them? (20:20) _____
_____

5. What did Paul testify to? (20:21) _____
_____

6. What did Paul not value? Why? (20:24) _____
_____

7. What was the purpose of Paul's ministry? (20:24) _____
_____

Paul's teaching to the elders (Acts 20:27-32)

8. What did Paul proclaim to them? (20:27) _____
_____

9. Who did Paul tell them to pay careful attention to? (20:28) _____
_____

10. What was the Church purchased with? (20:28b) Therefore, who owns the Church?
_____

11. Who would come into the church after Paul departed? (20:29) _____

_____

12. What would they do to the church? (20:29-30) _____

_____

13. Where would these fierce wolves come from? (20:30) _____

_____

14. What warning did Paul give these elders? (20:31) _____

_____

15. How did Paul warn them? (20:31) _____

_____

16. To who and what did Paul commend them to? (20:32) _____

_____

_____

Paul's model for the elders (Acts 20:33-35)

17. What did Paul not covet? Why? (20:33, 34) _____

_____

18. Why do you suppose that Paul worked? (20:34) _____

_____

19. What did Paul show them by working? Why? (20:35) _____

_____

_____

Paul's relationship with the elders (Acts 20:36-38)

20. What did Paul do with the elders when he was leaving them? (20:36) _____

_____

21. Describe Paul's relationship with the elders. (20:37-38) _____

_____

_____

Lesson 13
Apostles Developed Other Apostles • Acts 16:1–20:31; 1 Timothy; 2 Timothy; Titus

Paul selected apostles who were tested in the church (Acts 16:2-5)

1. What was the name of the disciple Paul met when he came to Lystra? (16:1) _____

   _____

2. Where did Timothy's faith first live? (2 Timothy 1:5) _____

   _____

3. Why do you think Paul chose Timothy? (Acts 16:2) _____

   _____

4. What did Paul want to do with Timothy? (16:3) _____

   _____

5. How did Paul train Timothy? (16:3-4) _____

   _____

6. What was the result of this training process? (16:5) _____

   _____

Paul built teams of people to assist him (Acts 18:24-28; 20:4-31)

7. Who were some of Paul's helpers? (18:24-28) _____

   _____

8. How were they trained in sound doctrine? (18:24-26) _____

   _____

9. Describe their effectiveness in the ministry of the Word. (18:27-28) _____

   _____

10. What is the difference in training for the ministry and training in the ministry? (20:4, 18, 31) Which is the most effective training? Why? _____

_____

Paul's instructions emphasized Timothy's character (1 and 2 Timothy)

11. Read through these letters (1 and 2 Timothy) and underline or highlight the words in your Bible that Paul uses to describe a leader's character as well as being a model and example of Christ. List some of these characteristics: _____

_____

_____

12. Go back and look at Barnabas' character on Lesson 10, questions 1-10 and list as many character traits as you can about Barnabas. You will be amazed the Bible has so much to say about him! _____

_____

13. Why is character so important in the apostle's and leader's ministry? (2 Timothy 2:20-22)

_____

_____

Paul used apostles to establish existing churches (Titus)

14. Why did Paul leave Titus in Crete? (1:5) _____

_____

15. What does it mean to "set in order"? (1:5-9) _____

_____

16. What did Paul tell Titus to teach? (2:1) _____

_____

17. Describe what Paul meant by "sound doctrine" or teaching. (2:2ff) _____

_____

Lesson 14
Apostles Trained for the Next Generation • 2 Timothy

Training faithful men (2 Timothy 2:2)

1. What types of men were entrusted with Paul's teaching? (2:2) _____

_____

2. What should they be enabled to do? (2:2) _____

_____

Timothy's charge (2 Timothy 4:1-5)

3. What did Paul charge Timothy to do? (4:1-5) _____

_____

4. Why is this charge so important? (4:1-5) _____

_____

Paul's farewell (2 Timothy 4:6-18)

5. What was Paul's perspective on his past life? His future life? (4:6-9) _____

_____

_____

6. What happened to Demas, Paul's disciple? (4:9-10) _____

_____

7. Based on Acts 15:37-40, why would Paul now want Mark? (4:11) _____

_____

_____

8. How did Paul handle the situation with Alexander? (4:14-15) What can you learn from Paul's
   dealings with Alexander? _____

_____

Lesson 15
God Calls and Chooses Unlikely Leaders

God does not call and choose His leaders based on the world's standard or criteria. For example, when Jesus chose the Twelve Disciples for His Father's very important task, He chose no one from the "religious establishment". To be sure, throughout the Bible, God's way of choosing leadership is much different than the ways of man and the world.

1. What type of brothers did God not call according to 1 Corinthians 1:26? _____
   _____
   _____

2. Who did God choose according to 1 Corinthians 1:27-28? _____
   _____
   _____

3. Why does God call and choose this type of person according to 1 Corinthians 1:29? _____
   _____
   _____

4. What was Gideon doing when the angel of the Lord appeared to him according to Judges 6:11?
   _____
   _____
   _____

5. How did Gideon respond to God's call according to Judges 6:12-15? _____
   _____
   _____

6. How did God respond to Gideon according to Judges 6:16? _____
   _____
   _____

7. Why were just 32,000 men too many to fight hundreds of thousands of Midianites according to
   Judges 7:2? _____
   _____

8. How many men did God finally leave Gideon to fight with according to Judges 7:7? _____

_____

9. What were some of the excuses Moses used in response to God's calling according to Exodus 3:11; 4:1, 10, 13? _____

_____

10. How did God respond to Moses according to Exodus 3:12; 4:11, 12? _____

_____

_____

11. Why did God choose David? He was just a shepherd boy, the last of Jesse's eight sons. Why did God not choose one of the other sons? (I Samuel 16:6-13) _____

_____

_____

12. What is the difference in how God chooses and how the world chooses? (I Samuel 16:7)

_____

_____

13. How did the elders, the scribes, and the high priest perceive Peter and John in Acts 4:13?

_____

_____

14. What did they realize or recognize about Peter and John in Acts 4:13? _____

_____

_____

Lesson 16
Powerful Leaders are Tested and Proven by God

Throughout Scripture we see leaders who were powerfully used by God, were first tested and proven. Activity and knowledge are no substitute for being tested for usefulness, purity and power. We are to rejoice in our tests and weaknesses so that we will experience purity with greater power and usefulness for God's glory.

1. What came to rest on Jesus after His baptism according to Matthew 3:16? _____

    _____

    _____

2. Where did the Holy Spirit immediately lead Jesus after His baptism according to Matthew 4:1?

    _____

3. After Jesus passed this time of testing in the wilderness, what did He begin to do according to

    Matthew 4:17? _____

    _____

4. Moses lived a total of 120 years. After his first 40 years of growing up in Egypt, who did Moses

    become according to Exodus 2:10? _____

    _____

5. Where did Moses spend his next 40 years according to Exodus 2:15? _____

    _____

    _____

6. What did he do while in the desert land according to Exodus 3:1? _____

    _____

7. Having passed his "desert test", how did Moses spend his final 40 years according Exodus

    3:10ff? _____

    _____

8. What did Peter say after Jesus declared they would all fall away according to Mark 14:26-31?

    _____

    _____

    _____

9. What happened when Peter failed his test according to Mark 14:72? _____

_____

_____

10. What was the result of Peter enduring his test according to Acts 2:38-41? _____

_____

_____

11. How did the Thessalonians receive the Word according to 1 Thessalonians 1:6? _____

_____

_____

12. What was the result of their testing or affliction according to 1 Thessalonians 1:7-8? _____

_____

_____

13. Why was Paul tested according to 2 Corinthians 12:7? _____

_____

_____

14. Describe Paul's thorn that was given to him? (2 Corinthians 12:7) _____

_____

_____

15. Instead of removal, what did the Lord give to Paul according to 2 Corinthians 12:9? _____

_____

_____

16. What makes God's power perfect in the believer? (2 Corinthians 12:9) _____

_____

17. Therefore, why did Paul boast about his weaknesses? (2 Corinthians 12:9) _____

_____

18. So, what were some things that Paul was content with and even delighted in according to
    2 Corinthians 12:10? _____

_____

Lesson 17
Key People in Paul's Life

Paul surrounded himself with key people who contributed to his success in taking the gospel to the Gentiles. Every person in Paul's life was useful and strategic in shaping this master church planter and man of God. You too will need these people in your life to shape your church planting success.

1. How do you think God used Stephen in Paul's conversion according to Acts 7:58-60?

   _____

   _____

2. What role do you think Barnabas played in Paul's life according to Acts 9:26-27 and 11:25-26?

   _____

   _____

3. What was Timothy's involvement and role in Paul's life according to 1 and 2 Timothy?

   _____

   _____

4. What role did Mark play in Paul's life and ministry according to 2 Timothy 4:10? How do you suppose this came about since Mark and Paul had separated? _____

   _____

   _____

5. Why do you think Paul had Luke with him according to 2 Timothy 4:11? _____

   _____

   _____

6. How did Titus help Paul according to 2 Timothy 4:10 and Titus 1:5? _____

   _____

   _____

7. Why would Paul mention Demas in his final words to Timothy right before his execution? (2 Timothy 4:10) _____

   _____

8. Even more amazing, why do you think Paul mentions Alexander? (2 Timothy 4:14)

_____

_____

9. Almost everyone deserted Paul (2 Timothy 1:15; 4:16) but who stood by him according to
   2 Timothy 4:17-18)? Why? _____

_____

_____

10. Who did Paul want to receive honor, credit and attention for his life and ministry? (2 Timothy
    4:18b) _____

_____

Discussion: Do you have a Paul in your life? _____ Why do you need a Paul in your life?

_____

_____

_____

Do you have a Timothy in your life? _____ Why do you need a Timothy in your life?

_____

_____

_____

_____

Project G
Developing a Biblical Model of Leadership

1. Make an outline of the biblical model of leadership development using the supra-cultural and timeless principles we have learned from Scripture: _____

    _____

    _____

2. Compare the leadership development process of today's church with your outline above in 1.

    _____

    _____

3. Where do you and your church need to change? _____

    _____

    _____

4. What can you do to help make that happen? _____

    _____

    _____

    _____

5. Write a brief strategy of your leadership role and responsibility in your church. _____

    _____

    _____

    _____

    _____

Review chapter 1, 2, 3, and 4 before going on to chapter 5.

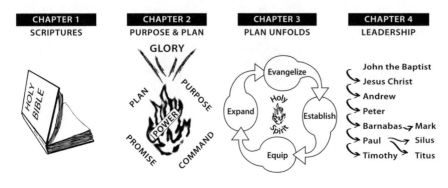

Chapter 5

OUR CHALLENGE

Develop Strong Churches

God's Plan for a Strong Church

Paul was a master church builder who laid the foundation upon which others built. He was not just concerned with starting new churches but also wanting existing churches to be strong. Look below at Paul's missionary journeys and see how many times he visited Iconium, Lystra, and Derbe? We know the first time was to preach the gospel, but why did he go back again, again and again?

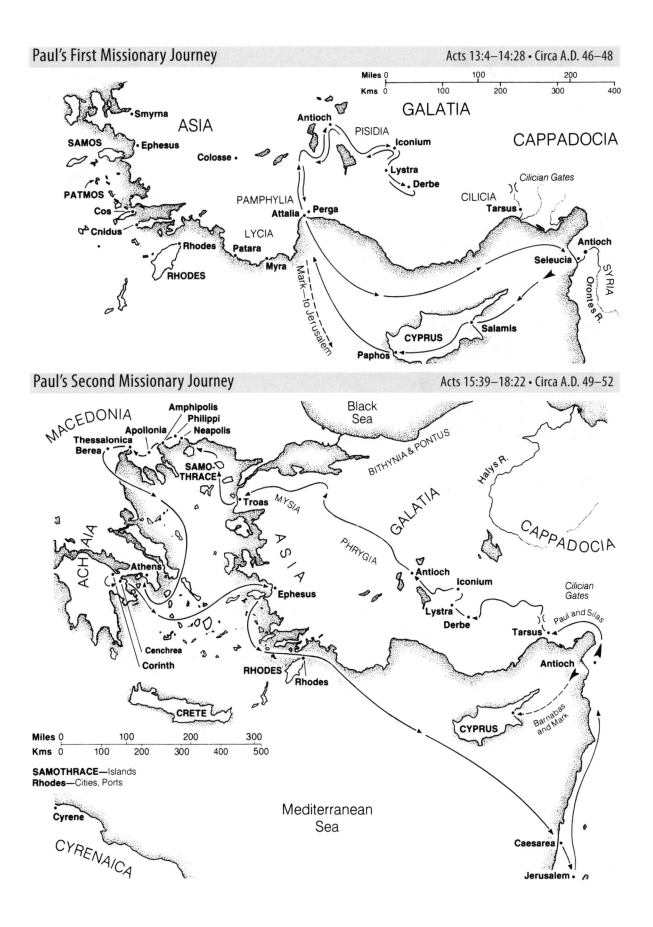

Paul's First Missionary Journey
Acts 13:4–14:28 • Circa A.D. 46–48

Miles 0 ... 100 ... 200
Kms 0 ... 100 ... 200 ... 300 ... 400

GALATIA

ASIA

CAPPADOCIA

- Smyrna
- Ephesus
- SAMOS
- Colosse
- PATMOS
- Cos
- Cnidus
- Rhodes
- RHODES
- Patara
- Myra

Antioch

PISIDIA
- Iconium
- Lystra
- Derbe

Cilician Gates

CILICIA
- Tarsus

PAMPHYLIA
- Attalia
- Perga

LYCIA

Mark—to Jerusalem

Antioch
- Seleucia
SYRIA
Orontes R.

Salamis
CYPRUS
Paphos

Paul's Second Missionary Journey
Acts 15:39–18:22 • Circa A.D. 49–52

Black Sea

MACEDONIA
- Amphipolis
- Philippi
- Apollonia
- Neapolis
- Thessalonica
- Berea
- SAMO-THRACE

BITHYNIA & PONTUS

GALATIA

Halys R.

CAPPADOCIA

Troas
MYSIA

ASIA

PHRYGIA

- Antioch
- Iconium
- Lystra
- Derbe

Cilician Gates

Paul and Silas

ACHAIA
- Athens

- Ephesus

Tarsus

Antioch

- Cenchrea
- Corinth

RHODES
- Rhodes

CRETE

Barnabas and Mark

CYPRUS

Miles 0 ... 100 ... 200 ... 300
Kms 0 ... 100 ... 200 ... 300 ... 400 ... 500

SAMOTHRACE—Islands
Rhodes—Cities, Ports

- Cyrene

CYRENAICA

Mediterranean Sea

- Caesarea

- Jerusalem

Paul's Third Missionary Journey

Acts 18:23–21:17 • Circa A.D. 53–57

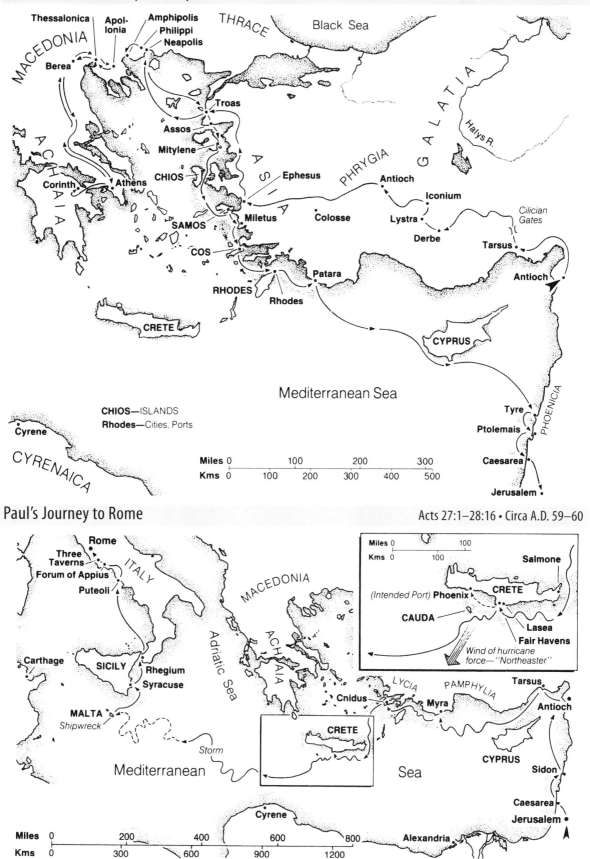

CHIOS—ISLANDS
Rhodes—Cities, Ports

Black Sea

THRACE

MACEDONIA

Thessalonica
Apol-lonia
Amphipolis
Philippi
Neapolis
Berea

Troas

Assos

Mitylene

ACHAIA

Corinth   Athens

CHIOS

Ephesus

PHRYGIA

GALATIA

Halys R.

Antioch

Iconium

Colosse

Lystra

Cilician Gates

Derbe

Tarsus

Miletus

SAMOS

COS

Patara

Antioch

RHODES

Rhodes

CRETE

CYPRUS

Mediterranean Sea

Cyrene

CYRENAICA

| Miles | 0 | 100 | 200 | 300 |
| Kms | 0 | 100 200 | 300 400 | 500 |

Tyre

Ptolemais

PHOENICIA

Caesarea

Jerusalem

Paul's Journey to Rome

Acts 27:1–28:16 • Circa A.D. 59–60

Rome
Three Taverns
Forum of Appius
Puteoli

ITALY

MACEDONIA

| Miles | 0 | 100 |
| Kms | 0 | 100 |

Salmone

(Intended Port) Phoenix   CRETE

CAUDA

Lasea

Fair Havens

Wind of hurricane force—"Northeaster"

Carthage

SICILY

Rhegium
Syracuse

Adriatic Sea

ACHAIA

MALTA
Shipwreck

Storm

Mediterranean

CRETE

Sea

LYCIA

PAMPHYLIA

Tarsus

Cnidus

Myra

Antioch

CYPRUS

Sidon

Cyrene

Caesarea

Alexandria

Jerusalem

Paul went back to these cities three more times for a total of four times; once to preach the gospel and three times to strengthen the disciples. Paul's concerns for strengthening is also evidenced by use of the word strengthen or establish in the following Scriptures:

By Luke: Acts 14:21-23; 15:36–16:5; 18:22-23

By Paul: Romans 1:8-15; 16:25-27; 1 Thessalonians 3:1-13; 2 Thessalonians 2:16-17

The words strengthen or establish is translated from the Greek word "sterizo" which means to fix or to fasten in place. Its usage gives us a key insight into what Paul wanted new churches to become. He wanted them to be doctrinally fixed or fastened in their faith. Literally this word means to support or to fix something so that it stands upright by itself or becomes immovable. For example, the original word literally was used to describe a stake that supports a vine. Look at the diagram below:

Therefore, Paul wanted the newly founded churches to be secure and stable, not easily moved or shaken by false doctrine or teaching. In order to strengthen the new disciples, Paul not only visited these churches, but he wrote letters to them.

Since Paul was the master church planter, let us consider his letters like tools of his trade, so to speak. Just as a master carpenter or mechanic must know what tools to use on a particular job so a master church planter should know what tools to use to make a church strong. See the tools in the diagram below and identify how each one is used:

While this seems so simple, it is amazing to see pastors, ministers and teachers using a hammer to saw a piece of wood or a saw to hammer a nail or a wrench to loosen a screw, etc. Just like carpenters and mechanics become masters of their trade so church leaders should become master church planters and establishers using God's tools which is His Word. God has given us every tool we need to deal with any construction or mechanical problem one might face in the church through His Word (2 Timothy 3:16-17). God has graciously and abundantly provided the necessary tools for us to make churches strong.

Paul's letters or tools to the churches can be chronologically and theologically divided into three categories: early letters, middle letters, and latter letters. This chronological order gives tremendous insights into the strategy Paul used to make these newly founded churches strong.

For example, his first or early letters or tools were written to establish new believers in the gospel of grace. The following is a breakdown or description of his letters in chronological order. (Note: Paul's letters or tools under the inspiration of the Holy Spirit addressed specific and real life issues in these newly founded or planted churches.)

Paul's Early Letters *(Tools used to establish and defend the gospel of grace)*

Galatians: Returning to the Spirit, faith and the pure gospel

1 and 2 Thessalonians: Standing firm in the gospel

1 Corinthians: Divisions solved by the implications of the gospel

2 Corinthians: Defense of the ministry and minister of the gospel

Romans: Preaching a complete discourse and work of the gospel

Paul's Middle Letters *(Tools for churches to be one-minded in the person and plan of Christ)*

Ephesians: Grasping the mystery of the church and revealing the plan of Christ

Philippians: Being of one mind in the church and the participation in the progress of the gospel

Colossians: Keeping the focus on Christ the Head of the church

Philemon: Relational implications of being one-minded in the progress of the gospel

Paul's Latter Letters *(Tools to put God's households in proper order)*

1 Timothy: Properly ordering the community life of the household of God, His church

Titus: Setting in order what remains by fully establishing the churches in sound doctrine

2 Timothy: Passing the baton on to well-trained, faithful leaders for the next generation

You could describe Paul's letters as building blocks, which were laid chronologically for the foundation of God's household. See the diagram below:

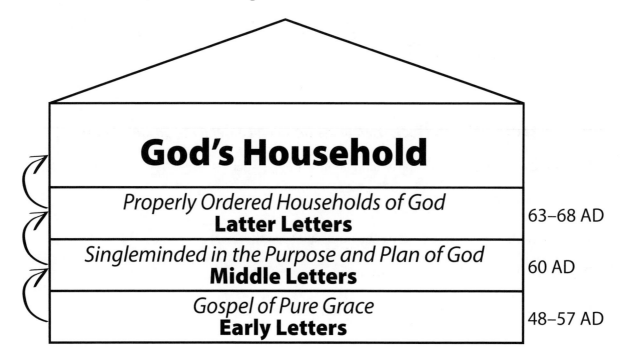

Lesson 18
Strengthening or Establishing Churches: Paul's Letters

Paul was a master church builder who laid the foundation upon which others built. He was not only concerned with starting new churches but he wanted existing churches to be strong and established. This is evidenced by the usage of "strengthen or establish" in the Word of God.

Stake
Church
Planter   new plant

Stand on its own   established plant

New Believer/Church   Established Believer/Church

Observation: Read and observe the following verses and write down what you learn about strengthening and establishing from the Word of God.

Example: Luke 22:32   *Jesus wanted Peter to <u>strengthen</u> his brothers but Peter would not be able to strengthen his brothers consistently until the <u>Holy Spirit</u> came to indwell him.*

1 Peter 1:22-25; 2 Peter 1:12 _____

_____

Acts 14:21-23 _____

_____

Acts 15:36–16:5 _____

_____

Acts 18:22-23 _____

_____

Romans 1:8-12 _____

_____

Romans16:25-27 _____

_____

1 Thessalonians 3:1-3 _____

_____

2 Thessalonians 2:16-17 _____

_____

2 Thessalonians 3:3 _____

_____

Revelation 3:1-2 _____

_____

Respond: Based on these verses, write a brief summary of the key principles and functions that you observed from God's Word that every person, family and church could follow at any time, in any culture. (Absolutes) _____

_____

Discussion: Contrast these principles with your life, family and church experience today.

_____

_____

_____

What changes do you need to make in your life, family and church here and now? _____

_____

_____

_____

Application: How and when will you make these changes in your life, family and church?

_____

_____

_____

Lesson 19
Establishing Churches: Paul's Early Letters 48–57AD

Galatians is one of Paul's first letters written to establish believers in the gospel of grace. This letter teaches that a believer is set free and justified by grace alone through faith. It exposes a popular substitute for the Spirit in today's church, which is the flesh.

Gospel of Pure Grace **Early Letters**

48–57 AD

Observation: Read and observe the following verses and write down what you learn about Paul's letter to the Galatians.

Example: Acts14:21-22 _After Paul and Barnabas preached the gospel in cities, they would return to each city to strengthen the disciples and encourage them to continue in the faith._

Galatians 1:1-5 _____

_____

_____

Galatians 1:6-10 _____

_____

_____

Galatians 1:11-24 _____

_____

_____

Galatians 2:1-10 _____

_____

Galatians 2:11-14 _____

_____

_____

Galatians 2:15-21 _____

_____

_____

Galatians 3:1-9 _____

_____

_____

Galatians 3:10-14 _____

_____

_____

Galatians 3:15-29 _____

_____

_____

Galatians 4:1-7 _____

_____

_____

Galatians 4:8-20 _____

_____

_____

Galatians 4:21-31 _____

_____

_____

Galatians 5:1-15 _____

_____

_____

Galatians 5:16-26 _____

_____

_____

Galatians 6:1-10 _____

_____

_____

Galatians 6:11-18 _____

_____

_____

Respond: Based on these verses, write a brief summary of the key principles and functions that you observed from God's Word that every person, family and church could follow at any time, in any culture. (Absolutes) _____

_____

_____

_____

Discussion: Contrast these principles with your life, family and church experience today. _____

_____

_____

_____

What changes do you need to make in your life, family and church here and now? _____

_____

_____

_____

Application: How and when will you make these changes in your life, family and church?

_____

_____

_____

_____

Lesson 20
Establishing Churches: Paul's Early Letters 48–57AD

1 and 2 Thessalonians was Paul's second and third letters written to establish believers in the gospel of grace. These letters encouraged new believers to persevere in their new faith, to continue to grow in their faith, and to live godly lives despite their afflictions and persecution.

Gospel of Pure Grace **Early Letters**

48–57 AD

Observation: Read and observe the following verses and write down what you learn about Paul's letters to the Thessalonians.

Example: Acts 14:21-22 _After Paul and Barnabas preached the gospel in cities, they would return to each city to strengthen the disciples and encourage them to continue in the faith._

1 Thessalonians 1:1-10 _____

_____

1 Thessalonians 2:1-16 _____

_____

1 Thessalonians 2:17–3:5 _____

_____

1 Thessalonians 3:6-13 _____

_____

1 Thessalonians 4:1-12 _____

_____

1 Thessalonians 4:13-18 _____

_____

1 Thessalonians 5:1-11 _____

_____

1 Thessalonians 5:12-28 _____

_____

2 Thessalonians 1:1-12 _____

_____

2 Thessalonians 2:1-12 _____

_____

2 Thessalonians 2:13-17 _____

_____

2 Thessalonians 3:1-5 _____

_____

2 Thessalonians 3:6-16 _____

_____

Respond: Based on these verses, write a brief summary of the key principles and functions that you observed from God's Word that every person, family and church could follow at any time, in any culture. (Absolutes) _____

_____

_____

Discussion: Contrast these principles with your life, family and church experience today.

_____

_____

What changes do you need to make in your life, family and church here and now? _____

_____

_____

_____

Application: How and when will you make these changes in your life, family and church?

_____

_____

_____

Lesson 21
Establishing Churches: Paul's Early Letters 48–57AD

First Corinthians was Paul's fourth letter written to establish new believers in the gospel of grace. This letter was written to unify and sanctify this new church by helping them to understand the implications of the gospel and to put into practice their position in Christ through the power of the Holy Spirit.

Gospel of Pure Grace **Early Letters** 　　48–57 AD

Observation: Read and observe the following verses and write down what you learn about Paul's letter to the Corinthians.

Example: Acts14:21-22 _After Paul and Barnabas preached the gospel in cities, they would <u>return to each city to strengthen</u> the disciples and <u>encourage</u> them to continue in the faith._

1 Corinthians 1:1-9 _____

_____

1 Corinthians 1:10-17 _____

_____

_____

1 Corinthians 1:18-31 _____

_____

1 Corinthians 2:1-5 _____

_____

_____

1 Corinthians 2:6-16 _____

_____

1 Corinthians 3:1-23 _____
_____
_____

1 Corinthians 4:1-21 _____
_____
_____

1 Corinthians 5:1-13 _____
_____
_____

1 Corinthians 6:1-11 _____
_____
_____

1 Corinthians 6:12-20 _____
_____
_____

1 Corinthians 7:1-16 _____
_____
_____

1 Corinthians 7:17-24 _____
_____
_____

1 Corinthians 7:25-40 _____
_____
_____

1 Corinthians 8:1-13 _____
_____
_____

1 Corinthians 9:1-27 _____
_____
_____

1 Corinthians 10:1-22 _____

_____

_____

1 Corinthians 10:23–11:1 _____

_____

_____

1 Corinthians 11:2-16 _____

_____

_____

1 Corinthians 11:17-34 _____

_____

_____

1 Corinthians 12:1-11 _____

_____

_____

1 Corinthians 12:12-31 _____

_____

_____

1 Corinthians 13:1-13 _____

_____

_____

1 Corinthians 14:1-25 _____

_____

_____

1 Corinthians 14:26-40 _____

_____

_____

1 Corinthians 15:1-11 _____

_____

_____

1 Corinthians 15:12-34 _____

_____

1 Corinthians 15:35-49 _____

_____

1 Corinthians 15:50-58 _____

_____

1 Corinthians 16:1-4 _____

_____

1 Corinthians 16:5-11 _____

_____

1 Corinthians 16:12-24 _____   _____

_____

Respond: Based on these verses, write a brief summary of the key principles and functions that you observed from God's Word that every person, family and church could follow at any time, in any culture. (Absolutes) _____

_____

_____

Discussion: Contrast these principles with your life, family and church experience today. _____

_____

_____

_____

What changes do you need to make in your life, family and church here and now? _____

_____

_____

_____

Application: How and when will you make these changes in your life, family and church?

_____

_____

_____

God's Plan for a Strong Church

Lesson 22
Establishing Churches: Paul's Early Letters 48–57AD

Second Corinthians was Paul's fifth letter written to establish new believers in the gospel of grace. False teachers were dividing the new church by discrediting both Paul and his message. So this letter was written to authenticate his message and to defend his apostleship.

Gospel of Pure Grace **Early Letters**

48–57 AD

Observation: Read and observe the following verses and write down what you learn about Paul's second letter to the Corinthians.

Example: Acts14:21-22   <u>After Paul and Barnabas preached the gospel in cities, they would return</u> <u>to each city to strengthen</u> the disciples and <u>encourage</u> them to continue in the faith.

2 Corinthians 1:1-11 _____

_____

2 Corinthians 1:12–2:4 _____

_____

_____

2 Corinthians 2:5-11 _____

_____

2 Corinthians 2:12-17 _____

_____

2 Corinthians 3:1-17 _____

_____

2 Corinthians 4:1-6 _____

_____

2 Corinthians 4:7-18 _____

_____

2 Corinthians 5:1-10 _____

_____

2 Corinthians 5:11–6:13 _____

_____

_____

2 Corinthians 6:14–7:1 _____

_____

_____

2 Corinthians 7:2-16 _____

_____

2 Corinthians 8:1-15 _____

_____

2 Corinthians 8:16-24 _____

_____

_____

2 Corinthians 9:1-5 _____

_____

_____

2 Corinthians 9:6-15 _____

_____

_____

2 Corinthians 10:1-18 _____

_____

_____

2 Corinthians 11:1-15 _____

_____

_____

2 Corinthians 11:16-33 _____

_____

_____

2 Corinthians 12:1-10 _____

_____

_____

2 Corinthians 12:11-21 _____

_____

_____

2 Corinthians 13:1-10 _____

_____

_____

2 Corinthians 13:11-14 _____

_____

_____

Respond: Based on these verses, write a brief summary of the key principles and functions that you observed from God's Word that every person, family and church could follow at any time, in any culture. (Absolutes) _____

_____

_____

Discussion: Contrast these principles with your life, family and church experience today.

_____

_____

_____

What changes do you need to make in your life, family and church here and now? _____

_____

_____

Application: How and when will you make these changes in your life, family and church?

_____

_____

_____

Lesson 23
Establishing Churches: Paul's Early Letters 48–57AD

Romans was Paul's sixth letter and his longest. It is the most complete treatise of the gospel and was written to establish new believers in the gospel of grace. Paul explains justification by faith alone and details the implications of sin, salvation, sanctification and service in Christ.

Gospel of Pure Grace **Early Letters**

48–57 AD

Observation: Read and observe the following verses and write down what you learn about Paul's letter to the Romans.

Example: Acts 14:21-22   *After Paul and Barnabas preached the gospel in cities, they would <u>return</u> <u>to each city to strengthen</u> the disciples and <u>encourage</u> them to continue in the faith.*

Romans 1:1-7 _____

_____

Romans 1:8-15 _____

_____

Romans 1:16-32 _____

_____

Romans 2:1-11 _____

_____

Romans 2:12-29 _____

_____

Romans 3:1-8 _____

_____

Romans 3:9-20 _____

_____

Romans 3:21-31 _____

_____

Romans 4:1-12 _____

_____

Romans 4:13-25 _____

_____

Romans 5:1-11 _____

_____

Romans 5:12-21 _____

_____

Romans 6:1-14 _____

_____

Romans 6:15-23 _____

_____

Romans 7:1-6 _____

_____

Romans 7:7-25 _____

_____

Romans 8:1-11 _____

_____

Romans 8:12-17 _____

_____

Romans 8:18-30 _____

_____

Romans 8:31-39 _____

_____

Romans 9:1-29 _____

_____

Romans 9:30–10:4 _____

_____

Romans 10:5-21 _____

_____

Romans 11:1-10 _____

_____

Romans 11:11-24 _____

_____

Romans 11:25-36 _____

_____

Romans 12:1-2 _____

_____

Romans 12:3-8 _____

_____

Romans 12:9-21 _____

_____

Romans 13:1-7 _____

_____

Romans 13:8-14 _____

_____

Romans 14:1-12 _____

_____

Romans 14:13-23 _____

_____

Romans 15:1-7 _____

_____

Romans 15:8-13 _____

_____

Romans 15:14-21 _____

_____

Romans 15:22-33 _____

_____

Romans 16:1-16 _____

_____

Romans 16:17-25 _____

_____

Respond: Based on these verses, write a brief summary of the key principles and functions that you observed from God's Word that every person, family and church could follow at any time, in any culture. (Absolutes) _____

_____

_____

Discussion: Contrast these principles with your life, family and church experience today.

_____

_____

_____

What changes do you need to make in your life, family and church here and now? _____

_____

_____

_____

Application: How and when will you make these changes in your life, family and church?

_____

_____

_____

Lesson 24
Establishing Churches: Paul's Middle Letters 60AD

Ephesians was Paul's first letter written from prison to establish and unify believers in the person and the eternal plan of Christ, which was hidden but now revealed. Paul explains how the gospel of grace impacts individuals and families in displaying God's glorious plan by His power at work in us.

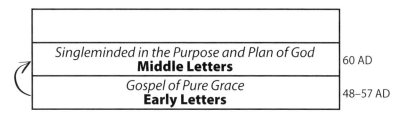

Singleminded in the Purpose and Plan of God **Middle Letters**	60 AD
Gospel of Pure Grace **Early Letters**	48–57 AD

Observation: Read and observe the following verses and write down what you learn about Paul's letter to the Ephesians.

Example: Acts 14:21-22 _After Paul and Barnabas preached the gospel in cities, they would <u>return to</u> <u>each city to strengthen</u> the disciples and <u>encourage</u> them to continue in the faith._

Ephesians 1:1-14 _____

_____

_____

Ephesians 1:15-23 _____

_____

_____

Ephesians 2:1-10 _____

_____

_____

Ephesians 2:11-22 _____

_____

Ephesians 3:1-13 _____

_____

_____

Ephesians 3:14-21 _____

_____

_____

Ephesians 4:1-16 _____

_____

_____

Ephesians 4:17-32 _____

_____

_____

Ephesians 5:1-21 _____

_____

_____

Ephesians 5:22-33 _____

_____

_____

Ephesians 6:1-4 _____

_____

_____

Ephesians 6:5-9 _____

_____

_____

Ephesians 6:10-20 _____

_____

_____

Ephesians 6:21-24 _____

_____

_____

Respond: Based on these verses, write a brief summary of the key principles and functions that you observed from God's Word that every person, family and church could follow at any time, in any culture. (Absolutes) _____

_____

_____

_____

Discussion: Contrast these principles with your life, family and church experience today.

_____

_____

_____

What changes do you need to make in your life, family and church here and now? _____

_____

_____

_____

Application: How and when will you make these changes in your life, family and church?

_____

_____

_____

Lesson 25
Establishing Churches: Paul's Middle Letters 60AD

Philippians was Paul's second letter written from prison to establish and unify believers in the person and the eternal plan of Christ. Paul explains how the gospel of grace and righteousness through faith impacts individuals and families to live as humble servants in Christ for the progress of the gospel.

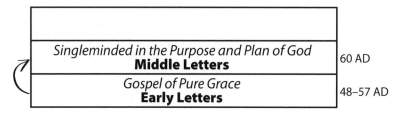

Singleminded in the Purpose and Plan of God **Middle Letters**	60 AD
Gospel of Pure Grace **Early Letters**	48–57 AD

Observation: Read and observe the following verses and write down what you learn about Paul's letter to the Philippians.

Example: Acts 14:21-22 _After Paul and Barnabas preached the gospel in cities, they would return to each city to strengthen the disciples and encourage them to continue in the faith._

Philippians 1:1-11 _____

_____

Philippians 1:12-18 _____

_____

Philippians 1:19-30 _____

_____

Philippians 2:1-11 _____

_____

Philippians 2:12-18 _____

_____

Philippians 2:19-30 _____

_____

Philippians 3:1-11 _____

_____

_____

Philippians 3:12–4:1 _____

_____

_____

Philippians 4:2-9 _____

_____

_____

Philippians 4:10-23 _____

_____

_____

Respond: Based on these verses, write a brief summary of the key principles and functions that you observed from God's Word that every person, family and church could follow at any time, in any culture. (Absolutes) _____

_____

_____

Discussion: Contrast these principles with your life, family and church experience today.

_____

_____

_____

What changes do you need to make in your life, family and church here and now? _____

_____

_____

_____

Application: How and when will you make these changes in your life, family and church?

_____

_____

_____

_____

Lesson 26
Establishing Churches: Paul's Middle Letters 60AD

Colossians was Paul's third letter written from prison to establish and unify believers in the person and the eternal plan of Christ, who is Head of the Church. Paul shows the superiority of Christ over philosophies, traditions and legalism, and how to live focused on the heavenly rather than the earthly.

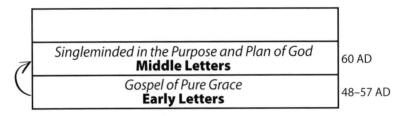

Singleminded in the Purpose and Plan of God **Middle Letters**	60 AD
Gospel of Pure Grace **Early Letters**	48–57 AD

Observation: Read and observe the following verses and write down what you learn about Paul's letter to the Colossians.

Example: Acts 14:21-22 *After Paul and Barnabas preached the gospel in cities, they would <u>return to each city to strengthen</u> the disciples and <u>encourage</u> them to continue in the faith.*

Colossians 1:1-14 _____

_____

_____

Colossians 1:15-23 _____

_____

_____

Colossians 1:24–2:5 _____

_____

_____

Colossians 2:6-15 _____

_____

_____

Colossians 2:16-23 _____

_____

_____

Colossians 3:1-17 _____

_____

_____

Colossians 3:18–4:1 _____

_____

_____

Colossians 4:2-6 _____

_____

_____

Colossians 4:7-18 _____

_____

_____

Respond: Based on these verses, write a brief summary of the key principles and functions that you observed from God's Word that every person, family and church could follow at any time, in any culture. (Absolutes) _____

_____

_____

Discussion: Contrast these principles with your life, family and church experience today.

_____

_____

_____

What changes do you need to make in your life, family and church here and now? _____

_____

_____

Application: How and when will you make these changes in your life, family and church?

_____

_____

_____

Lesson 27
Establishing Churches: Paul's Middle Letters 60AD

Philemon was Paul's fourth letter written from prison to establish and unify believers in the person and the eternal plan of Christ. Paul shows the power of the Gospel and its relational implications in individuals and families being one-minded in the progress of the gospel.

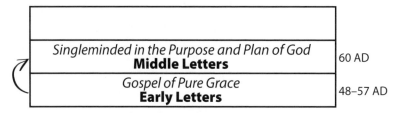

Singleminded in the Purpose and Plan of God **Middle Letters**	60 AD
Gospel of Pure Grace **Early Letters**	48–57 AD

Observation: Read and observe the following verses and write down what you learn about Paul's letter to Philemon.

Example: Acts 14:21-22 <u>After Paul and Barnabas preached the gospel in cities, they would <u>return to each city to strengthen</u> the disciples and <u>encourage</u> them to continue in the faith.</u>

Philemon 1:1-3 _____

_____

_____

_____

Philemon 1:4-7 _____

_____

_____

_____

Philemon 1:8-25 _____

_____

_____

_____

Respond: Based on these verses, write a brief summary of the key principles and functions that you observed from God's Word that every person, family and church could follow at any time, in any culture. (Absolutes) _____

_____

_____

Discussion: Contrast these principles with your life, family and church experience today.

_____

_____

_____

What changes do you need to make in your life, family and church here and now? _____

_____

_____

_____

Application: How and when will you make these changes in your life, family and church?

_____

_____

_____

Lesson 28
Establishing Churches: Paul's Latter Letters 63–68AD

First Timothy was Paul's first letter written to establish churches into a properly ordered household. Paul is passing on to his spiritual son, Timothy, the pattern needed for him to continue Paul's work after his departure. The pattern is sound teaching, godliness with contentment, and the appointment of qualified spiritual overseers.

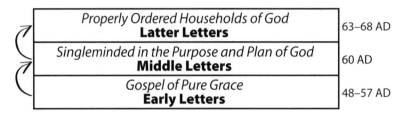

Properly Ordered Households of God **Latter Letters**	63–68 AD
Singleminded in the Purpose and Plan of God **Middle Letters**	60 AD
Gospel of Pure Grace **Early Letters**	48–57 AD

Observation: Read and observe the following verses and write down what you learn about Paul's letter to Timothy.

Example: 1 Timothy 3:14-15; Titus1:5 <u>Paul wrote to Timothy how one ought to behave in the</u> <u>household of God, the church of the living God, He left Titus in Crete to set the church in order.</u>

1 Timothy 1:1-11 _____

_____

1 Timothy 1:12-20 _____

_____

1 Timothy 2:1-15 _____

_____

1 Timothy 3:1-7 _____

_____

1 Timothy 3:8-13 _____

_____

1 Timothy 3:14-16 _____

_____

1 Timothy 4:1-5 _____

_____

1 Timothy 4:6-16 _____

_____

_____

1 Timothy 5:1–6:2 _____

_____

_____

1 Timothy 6:3-10 _____

_____

_____

1 Timothy 6:11-21 _____

_____

_____

Respond: Based on these verses, write a brief summary of the key principles and functions that you observed from God's Word that every person, family and church could follow at any time, in any culture. (Absolutes) _____

_____

_____

Discussion: Contrast these principles with your life, family and church experience today.

_____

_____

_____

What changes do you need to make in your life, family and church here and now? _____

_____

_____

_____

Application: How and when will you make these changes in your life, family and church?

_____

_____

_____

Lesson 29
Establishing Churches: Paul's Latter Letters 63–68AD

Titus was Paul's second letter written to establish churches into a properly ordered household. Paul is teaching what accords with sound doctrine, which is the proper ordering of God's household in the different biblical roles. He explains the importance of living by grace and maintaining purity in God's household.

Properly Ordered Households of God **Latter Letters**	63–68 AD
Singleminded in the Purpose and Plan of God **Middle Letters**	60 AD
Gospel of Pure Grace **Early Letters**	48–57 AD

Observation: Read and observe the following verses and write down what you learn about Paul's letter to Titus.

Example: 1 Timothy 3:14-15; Titus 1:5 *Paul wrote to Timothy how one ought <u>to behave in the</u> <u>household of God, the church of the living God.</u> He left Titus in Crete to set <u>the church in order.</u>*

Titus 1:1-4 _____

_____

_____

Titus 1:5-16 _____

_____

_____

Titus 2:1-15 _____

_____

_____

Titus 3:1-11 _____

_____

_____

Titus 3:12-15 _____

_____

_____

Respond: Based on these verses, write a brief summary of the key principles and functions that you observed from God's Word that every person, family and church could follow at any time, in any culture. (Absolutes) _____

_____

_____

_____

Discussion: Contrast these principles with your life, family and church experience today.

_____

_____

_____

What changes do you need to make in your life, family and church here and now? _____

_____

_____

_____

Application: How and when will you make these changes in your life, family and church?

_____

_____

_____

Lesson 30
Establishing Churches: Paul's Latter Letters 63-68AD

Second Timothy was Paul's last letter written from prison, prior to his execution, to establish churches into properly ordered households. Paul is passing on to his spiritual son the importance of entrusting the Word to faithful leaders who will be able to entrust it to others.

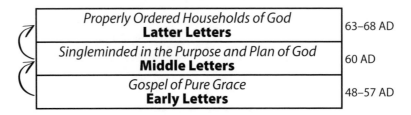

Properly Ordered Households of God **Latter Letters**	63–68 AD
Singleminded in the Purpose and Plan of God **Middle Letters**	60 AD
Gospel of Pure Grace **Early Letters**	48–57 AD

Observation: Read and observe the following verses and write down what you learn about Paul's last letter to Timothy.

Example: 1 Timothy 3:14-15; Titus 1:5 _Paul wrote to Timothy how one ought to behave in the household of God, the church of the living God. He left Titus in Crete to set the church in order._

2 Timothy 1:1-18 _____

_____

_____

2 Timothy 2:1-13 _____

_____

_____

2 Timothy 2:14-26 _____

_____

_____

2 Timothy 3:1-9 _____

_____

_____

2 Timothy 3:10-17 _____

_____

_____

2 Timothy 4:1-8 _____

_____

_____

2 Timothy 4:9-18 _____

_____

_____

2 Timothy 4:19-22 _____

_____

Respond: Based on these verses, write a brief summary of the key principles and functions that you observed from God's Word that every person, family and church could follow at any time, in any culture. (Absolutes) _____

_____

_____

_____

Discussion: Contrast these principles with your life, family and church experience today.

_____

_____

_____

What changes do you need to make in your life, family and church here and now? _____

_____

_____

_____

Application: How and when will you make these changes in your life, family and church?

_____

_____

_____

Project H
How to Fully Establish a Church

1. Write a one paragraph summary of Paul's concept of the "establishing" process.

   _____

   _____

   _____

   _____

   _____

2. Summarize how each of Paul's groups of letters (Early, Middle, and Latter) contributed to the establishing process.

   Early Letters: _____

   _____

   _____

   _____

   Middle Letters: _____

   _____

   _____

   _____

   Latter Letters: _____

   _____

   _____

   _____

3. Begin to develop in writing or diagram or chart, a strategy for fully establishing a church. This is a living project, which will be modified as the course is completed.

   _____

   _____

   _____

   _____

   _____

God's Plan for a Strong Church

Lesson 31
An Established Church Defined Biblically

Paul was a master church builder who laid the foundation upon which others built. He was not just concerned with starting new churches; he wanted existing churches to be strong and established. What does an established church look like according to the Word of God? See diagram below:

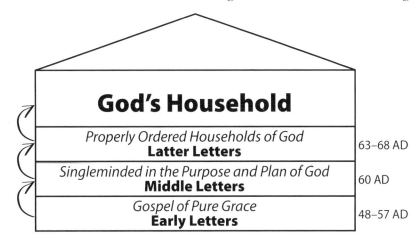

Observation: Read and observe the following verses and write down what you learn about an established church from the Word of God.

Example: Acts 1:8 *One who is filled with the power of the Holy Spirit and being a witness from their Jerusalem to the world.*

Acts 2:37-39 _____

_____

Acts 2:42-47 _____

_____

Acts 13:1-3 _____

_____

Acts 14:21-23 _____

_____

Acts 20:17-38 _____

_____

_____

1 Corinthians 13:1-13 _____

_____

Ephesians 1:15-18 _____

_____

Colossians 1:3-6 _____

_____

1 Thessalonians 1:2-4 _____

_____

2 Thessalonians 1:3-4 _____

_____

1 Corinthians 13:13 _____

_____

Respond: Based on these verses, write a brief summary of the key principles and functions that you observed from God's Word that every person, family and church could follow at any time, in any culture. (Absolutes) _____

_____

_____

Discussion: Contrast these principles with your life, family and church experience today.

_____

_____

_____

What changes do you need to make in your life, family and church here and now? _____

_____

_____

_____

Application: How and when will you make these changes in your life, family and church?

_____

_____

_____

God's Plan for a Strong Church

Project I
Establishing a New Testament Church

1. Describe a New Testament established church. Begin your description with, "A New Testament established church is…" Be certain the basic core elements are true for all churches at any time, in any culture. A New Testament established church is: _____

   _____

   _____

   _____

2. Compare your church with your description of a New Testament established church. Where does your church need to change? _____

   _____

   _____

   _____

3. What can you do to help change today's church into more of a New Testament model?

   _____

   _____

   _____

4. Write a brief strategy of your role and responsibility in helping strengthen or renew your church to the biblical model:

   _____

   _____

   _____

Review chapter 1, 2, 3, 4, and 5 before going to chapter 6.

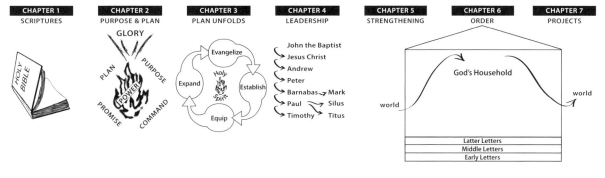

Chapter 6

OUR CHALLENGE

Develop Ordered Churches

Now we want to look at God's eternal plan for the age which is a basis for ALL strategies and plans and purposes in God's household. His household or Church is made up of families which are made up of individuals. The following diagram illustrates God's design for His Eternal Plan:

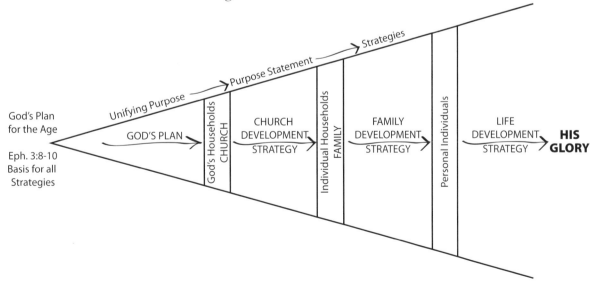

Within God's Plan, Paul had a Twofold Ministry

The Apostle Paul states in Ephesians 3:1-12 that his ministry is basically twofold:

1. What was Paul's first part of his twofold ministry according to Ephesians 3:8?

_____

_____

2. What was Paul's second part of his twofold ministry according to Ephesians 3:9? _____

_____

Paul not only wanted to preach the "unsearchable riches of Christ"; he wanted to reveal or make known the "administration or stewardship" of God's plan. Making known this plan was equally as important as preaching the gospel. Therefore, let us look further into the meaning of this key word of administration, steward-ship or plan that Paul used here. The word administration or plan in the Greek is *"oikonomia"* which is a compound word that comes from two words:

"oikos" which means house, household, family, or home

"nomos" which means law or order

Therefore, *"oikonomia"* means house law or household order. In addition to preaching the gospel of grace, Paul's job included revealing or making known God's order for his family or household, which is made up of both Jews and Gentiles. Paul clearly understood his job to be one of declaring how God wanted His church structured and how it was to function. This theme runs continuously and consistently throughout Paul's letters. When Paul writes to Timothy and Titus, he is instructing the believers how to properly live within the household or family of God, the church (1 Timothy 3:14-15). This concept of family is a universal concept since everyone knows about a family. It is important to under-stand that the church is a family made up of individual families. In other words, God's household or family is made up of many individual households or families; therefore, order in the church or household of God flows from order in the family. Proper order in the family will provide good order in the church. Disorder in the family will affect the order in the church. Peace, harmony, and unity in the family will be enhanced when everyone follows Paul's instructions and fulfills his or her biblical roles in the family and church.

Paul expected believers to follow these instructions he established for churches. He presented these instructions or principles in the thirteen letters he wrote to the various churches and individuals. These churches, which had not yet fully fol-lowed his instruction, were considered as needing to be set in order. This is why Paul told Titus to stay in Crete according to Titus 1:5.

Paul's latter letters to Timothy and Titus were written to give us these household management instructions. Ministry in the church should be complementary and not conflicting with the family, just as women complement men, deacons complement elders, and elders complement Christ. No one should be at odds with anyone in ministry at home or church. It is all interrelated and connected. For instance, according to 1 Timothy 3:4-5 and Titus 1:6 if a man can't manage his home, he might not be qualified to manage the church. Strong biblical leadership in the church comes from strong biblical leadership in the home.

Looking at relationships in the home helps us see our roles and responsibilities more clearly and with more sincerity in the church. Since the church is a family and not a business, knowing our role and responsibilities at home will enhance our church structure and function. Let's see what Paul has to say about the individual and family as they function together within the family of families or the household of God.

God's Plan for an Ordered Church

This diagram shows the progression of an ordered church found in Lessons 33–46.

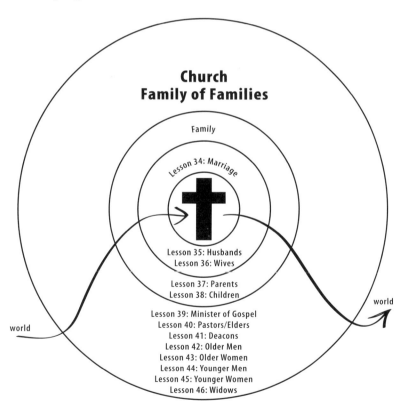

**Church
Family of Families**

Family

Lesson 34: Marriage

Lesson 35: Husbands
Lesson 36: Wives

Lesson 37: Parents
Lesson 38: Children

Lesson 39: Minister of Gospel
Lesson 40: Pastors/Elders
Lesson 41: Deacons
Lesson 42: Older Men
Lesson 43: Older Women
Lesson 44: Younger Men
Lesson 45: Younger Women
Lesson 46: Widows

world

world

You can see Christ should be made known and seen by the world through our individual lives, our marriage, our family and our church and by the same token, the world should see Christ through our church, our family, our marriages and our individual lives. They are all interrelated and a breakdown in any of these relationships affects all the relationships and will reveal the wrong image of the Bride of Christ to the world.

Biblical Roles in the Church Families

Lesson 32
Household Family Order

The church is God's family or household, which is made up of many families or individual households (see diagram below). Paul writes to Timothy and Titus explaining to them how to instruct churches to live properly in the household of God, the church.

Family of Families

Observation: Read and observe the following verses and write down what you learn about living in God's household.

Example: Ephesians 3:8-10   _Paul not only preached the riches of Christ but he <u>revealed</u> for every-_
one <u>God's Household order</u> so God's <u>manifold wisdom</u> would <u>be made known</u>.

Genesis 18:19 _____

_____

Genesis 35:2-5 _____

_____

Matthew 12:25 _____

_____

1 Peter 4:17 _____

_____

Romans 12:4-5 _____

_____

1 Corinthians 11:3 _____

_____

1 Corinthians 12:1-26 _____

_____

Ephesians 2:19-20 _____

_____

Ephesians 2:21-22 _____

_____

1 Timothy 3:4-5 _____

_____

1 Timothy 3:14-15 _____

_____

Titus 1:5 _____

_____

Titus 2:1 _____

_____

Respond: Based on these verses, write a brief summary of the key principles and functions that you observed from God's Word that every person, family and church could follow at any time, in any culture. (Absolutes) _____

_____

_____

Discussion: Contrast these principles with your life, family and church experience today.

_____

_____

What changes do you need to make in your life, family and church here and now? _____

_____

_____

_____

Application: How and when will you make these changes in your life, family and church?

_____

_____

_____

Lesson 33
Your Life in Christ

One of the greatest and most important privileges a believer has is to walk personally in the presence of Christ and God the Father by the power of the Holy Spirit. This awesome privilege is often neglected, yet it is the one relationship that every believer is invited and entitled to participate in.

**Church
Family of Families**

Observation: Read and observe the following verses and write down what you learn about your relationship with Christ.

Example: 1 Timothy 3:14-15 *Paul writes to Timothy on how <u>one ought to behave</u> in the <u>household of God,</u> which is the <u>church of the living God,</u> a pillar and buttress of truth.*

Genesis 3:8-9 _____

_____

_____

Genesis 5:24 _____

_____

_____

Genesis 48:15 _____

_____

_____

Joshua 1:8 _____

_____

Psalm 5:3 _____

Matthew 6:33 _____

Mark 1:35 _____

Mark 3:13-14 _____

Luke 10:38-42 _____

Luke 15:3-32 _____

John 15:1-11 _____

John 21:15-19 _____

Acts 4:13 _____

Acts 20:28 _____

Galatians 6:14-15 _____

Romans 12:1-2 _____

1 Corinthians 2:2 _____

Philippians 3:7-14 _____

1 John 1:3-7 _____

_____

Revelation 3:20 _____

_____

Respond: Based on these verses, write a brief summary of the key principles and functions that you observed from God's Word that every person, family and church could follow at any time, in any culture. (Absolutes) _____

_____

_____

_____

Discussion: Contrast these principles with your life, family and church experience today.

_____

_____

_____

_____

What changes do you need to make in your life, family and church here and now? _____

_____

_____

_____

Application: How and when will you make these changes in your life, family and church?

_____

_____

_____

_____

Lesson 34
The Role of Marriage

The Church has allowed culture to redefine marriage. The Word of God defines marriage as a sacred vow between a man and a woman. By going back to the Word, husbands and wives can recapture the biblical view of marriage as it relates to the Body of Christ, the church.

Church
Family of Families

Observation: Read and observe the following verses and write down what you learn about God's view of Marriage.

Example: 1 Timothy 3:14-15 <u>Paul writes to Timothy on how <u>one ought to behave</u> in the <u>household of God,</u> which is the <u>church of the living God,</u> a pillar and buttress of truth.</u>

Genesis 2:18-25 _____

_____

Matthew 19:3-6 _____

_____

Mark 10:6-9 _____

_____

Luke 20:34-35 _____

_____

1 Corinthians 7:1-16 _____

_____

_____

1 Corinthians 13:4-13 _____

_____

Ephesians 3:8-11 _____

_____

Ephesians 5:29-33 _____

_____

Colossians 3:18-23 _____

_____

Hebrews 13:4-6 _____

_____

_____

Respond: Based on these verses, write a brief summary of the key principles and functions that you observed from God's Word that every person, family and church could follow at any time, in any culture. (Absolutes) _____

_____

_____

_____

Discussion: Contrast these principles with your life, family and church experience today.

_____

_____

_____

What changes do you need to make in your life, family and church here and now? _____

_____

_____

_____

Application: How and when will you make these changes in your life, family and church?

_____

_____

_____

_____

Lesson 35
The Role of Husbands

The Word of God clearly gives the headship of the home to the husband who submits to Christ. His role is to love, guide, protect and provide spiritual and physical leadership for his wife and family. This role is an essential key to his ministry and a qualification to be an overseer of the Church.

Church
Family of Families

Observation: Read and observe the following verses and write down what you learn about the role of husbands.

Example: 1 Timothy 3:14-15   *Paul writes to Timothy on how <u>one ought to behave</u> in the <u>household of God,</u> which is the <u>church of the living God,</u> a pillar and buttress of truth.*

Genesis 2:15-24 _____

_____

Genesis 3:1-7 _____

_____

Genesis 3:8-20 _____

_____

Jeremiah 44:19-23 _____

_____

1 Corinthians 11:3 _____

_____

_____

1 Corinthians 14:33-40 _____

_____

Ephesians 5:21 _____

_____

Ephesians 5:23-24 _____

_____

Ephesians 5:25 _____

_____

Ephesians 5:26 _____

_____

Ephesians 5:27 _____

_____

Ephesians 5:28-30 _____

_____

Ephesians 5:31-32 _____

_____

_____

Ephesians 5:33 _____

_____

_____

Colossians 3:19 _____

_____

_____

1 Timothy 3:1-6 _____

_____

_____

1 Peter 3:7 and 2:18-3:9 _____

_____

_____

Respond: Based on these verses, write a brief summary of the key principles and functions that you observed from God's Word that every person, family and church could follow at any time, in any culture. (Absolutes) _____

_____

_____

_____

Discussion: Contrast these principles with your life, family and church experience today.

_____

_____

_____

_____

What changes do you need to make in your life, family and church here and now? _____

_____

_____

_____

_____

Application: How and when will you make these changes in your life, family and church?

_____

_____

_____

_____

_____

Lesson 36
The Role of Wives

Proverbs says, "An excellent wife, who can find? For her worth is far above jewels." Her role is often misaligned by culture but when Scripture is followed under the control of the Holy Spirit, she has a beautiful union with her husband. Her role is absolutely essential to her husband's ministry and spiritual condition.

**Church
Family of Families**

Observation: Read and observe the following verses and write down what you learn about the role of wives.

Example: 1 Timothy 3:14-15 <u>Paul writes to Timothy on how <u>one ought to behave</u> in the <u>household</u> of God,</u> which is the <u>church of the living God,</u> a pillar and buttress of truth.

Genesis 2:15-24 _____

_____

Genesis 3:1-7 _____

_____

Genesis 3:8-20 _____

_____

Proverbs 19:14 _____

_____

Proverbs 31:10-31 _____

_____

Jeremiah 44:19-23 _____

_____

1 Corinthians 7:1-5 _____

_____

1 Corinthians 14:33-40 _____

_____

Ephesians 5:21-24 _____

_____

Colossians 3:18 _____

_____

1 Timothy 3:11 _____

_____

Titus 2:3-5 _____

_____

1 Peter 3:1-6 and 2:18–3:9 _____

_____

Respond: Based on these verses, write a brief summary of the key principles and functions that you observed from God's Word that every person, family and church could follow at any time, in any culture. (Absolutes) _____

_____

Discussion: Contrast these principles with your life, family and church experience today.

_____

_____

What changes do you need to make in your life, family and church here and now? _____

_____

_____

Application: How and when will you make these changes in your life, family and church?

_____

_____

Lesson 37
The Role of Parents

Society, and now the church, are flooded with all kinds of books and intellectual experts on parenting. But for the most important process in society, parenting, there is very little teaching from the Scriptures. Yet, parenting and managing the home is an important qualification to be a pastor/elder in the church.

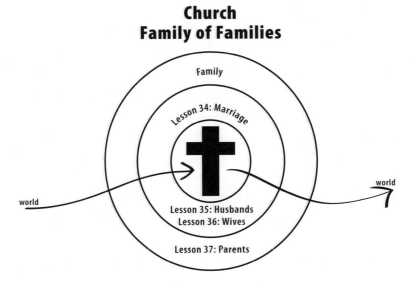

Church Family of Families

Observation: Read and observe the following verses and write down what you learn about parenting from the Word of God.

Example: 1 Timothy 3:14-15 _Paul writes to Timothy on how one ought to behave in the household of God, which is the church of the living God, a pillar and buttress of truth._

Genesis 1:26–3:24 _____

_____

_____

Genesis 22:1-14 _____

_____

_____

Deuteronomy 6:4-9 _____

_____

_____

Proverbs 13:24 _____

_____

_____

Proverbs 17:6 _____

_____

_____

Proverbs 19:14 _____

_____

_____

Proverbs 22:6 _____

_____

_____

Malachi 4:5-6 _____

_____

_____

John 9:1-3 _____

_____

_____

Romans 1:30 _____

_____

_____

Ephesians 6:1-4 _____

_____

_____

Colossians 3:20-21 _____

_____

_____

2 Timothy 3:2 _____

_____

_____

Respond: Based on these verses, write a brief summary of the key principles and functions that you observed from God's Word that every person, family and church could follow at any time, in any culture. (Absolutes) _____

_____

_____

_____

Discussion: Contrast these principles with your life, family and church experience today.

_____

_____

_____

_____

What changes do you need to make in your life, family and church here and now? _____

_____

_____

_____

_____

Application: How and when will you make these changes in your life, family and church?

_____

_____

_____

_____

Lesson 38
The Role of Children

The world and culture today encourages children to disregard and disrespect their parents. The Word of God makes it perfectly clear that parents are to be obeyed and respected. Many times this respect is difficult but this commandment, if obeyed, promises a full life.

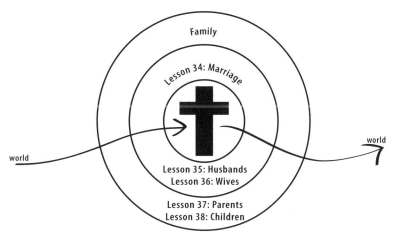

**Church
Family of Families**

Observation: Read and observe the following verses and write down what you learn about the role of children.

Example: 1 Timothy 3:14-15 *Paul writes to Timothy on how one ought to behave in the household of God, which is the church of the living God, a pillar and buttress of truth.*

1 Samuel 1:21–2:36 _____

_____

_____

Job 31:15 _____

_____

_____

Psalm 127:3 _____

_____

_____

Psalm 144:12 _____

_____

Proverbs 1:7-10 _____

_____

_____

Proverbs 4:1 _____

_____

_____

Proverbs 5:7 _____

_____

_____

Proverbs 17:6 _____

_____

_____

Proverbs 31:28 _____

_____

_____

Jeremiah 1:5 _____

_____

Mark 10:14-16 _____

_____

Luke 2:40, 52 _____

_____

Ephesians 6:1-3 _____

_____

Colossians 3:20 _____

_____

1 Timothy 5:4 _____

_____

2 Timothy 1:5, 3:15 _____

_____

Respond: Based on these verses, write a brief summary of the key principles and functions that you observed from God's Word that every person, family and church could follow at any time, in any culture. (Absolutes) _____

_____

_____

_____

Discussion: Contrast these principles with your life, family and church experience today.

_____

_____

_____

_____

What changes do you need to make in your life, family and church here and now? _____

_____

_____

_____

_____

Application: How and when will you make these changes in your life, family and church?

_____

_____

_____

_____

_____

Project J
Setting the Family in Order

1. Make an outline or diagram or chart of Paul's concept of managing individual families using the different roles and their responsibilities within the family.

Christ: _____

_____

_____

Marriage: _____

_____

_____

Husbands: _____

_____

_____

Wives: _____

_____

_____

Parents: _____

_____

_____

Children: _____

_____

_____

2. Compare your family to your outline or diagram in the above answer (1). Where does your family need to change? _____

_____

_____

_____

_____

3. What can you do to help make that happen? _____

_____

_____

_____

_____

4. Write a brief strategy of your role and responsibility in your family: _____

_____

_____

_____

_____

_____

_____

_____

Biblical Roles in the Church: the Family of Families

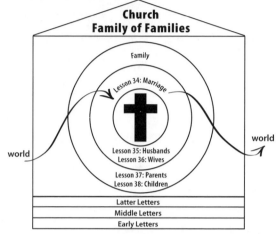

Now having set the family in order we transition to setting the family of families, the church, or household of God in order. As we have learned, order in the church flows from order in the family. This is a very simple principle to understand since most cultures are familiar with family. But even with this basic knowledge, family order is a major problem in most churches today. Practically every problem in the church is a reflection of a problem in the family. Therefore, it is imperative that the previous section pertaining to the family is in proper order before moving on to the church. Based on what you have learned, fill in the blanks in the following diagram.

Try to complete without looking back. This diagram will help you to understand the concept of the church order flowing out of the family order:

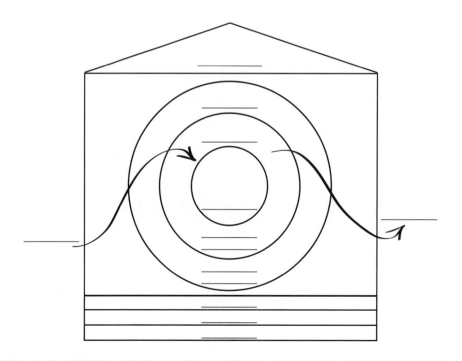

Biblical Roles in the Church Family

Lesson 39
The Role of Ministers of the Gospel

The Word of God clearly defines the function of the minister of the gospel or apostle (with a little "a") in the early church and there is *no* biblical reason to think or act like this role ended in the first century. They were responsible for laying new foundations and repairing the old foundation of God's household. This very important role has been diminished and hidden far too long, resulting in weak and stagnant churches. (Note: At the end of this lesson are two articles pertaining to this important role of an apostle. The first article gives a biblical description of the "minister of the gospel" and the second is concerning his "financial support".)

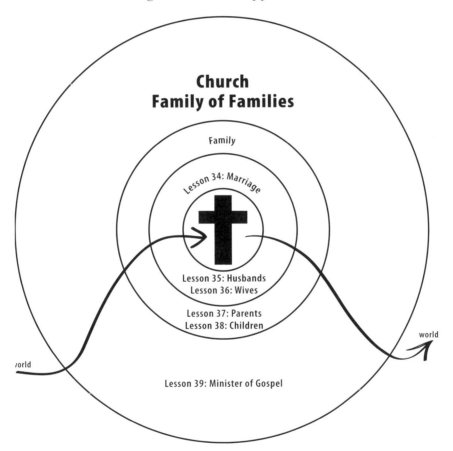

Observation: Read and observe the following verses and write down what you learn about the role of ministers of the gospel.

Example: 1 Timothy 3:14-15 <u>Paul writes to Timothy on how one ought to behave in the household of God,</u> which is the <u>church of the living God,</u> a pillar and buttress of truth.

Ephesians 3:7 _____

_____

Ephesians 4:11-14 _____

_____

1 Timothy 1:5-20 _____

_____

1 Timothy 2:1-7 _____

_____

Titus 1:5 _____

_____

2 Timothy 2:15-26 _____

_____

2 Timothy 4:1-7 _____

_____

Respond: Based on these verses, write a brief summary of the key principles and functions that you observed from God's Word that every person, family and church could follow at any time, in any culture. (Absolutes) _____

_____

_____

Discussion: Contrast these principles with your life, family and church experience today.

_____

_____

What changes do you need to make in your life, family and church here and now? _____

_____

_____

_____

Application: How and when will you make these changes in your life, family and church?

_____

_____

_____

Church Planter's Ministry Described Biblically

The ministry of church planters or apostles (with a small "a") did not end in the first century. Today they are often referred to as "missionaries" or "evangelists", or even "pastors", but do modern day definitions go far enough in explaining this special New Testament ministerial calling? These apostles were an extension of the church whose duties included *preaching* the gospel, *teaching* converts, and *establishing* the churches. Let us look at their responsibilities as revealed in the Antioch model of Evangelizing, Establishing, Equipping and Expanding.

The Church Planter's Ministry Described

Evangelizing:

The church planters founded churches by *preaching the gospel* and organizing the disciples into communities. Their teachings formed the believer's faith which was the foundation of the new church. At times, the church planters would have to do repair work on this foundation.

Establishing:

The apostle was to be devoted to establishing churches and *setting the churches in order* through teaching and preaching the truths of how a church, the household of God, ought to conduct itself. This was all done with a view of keeping the church on an orderly course (Titus 1:5; 1 Timothy 3:14-16; 6:2b; 1 Thessalonians 2:1–3:10).

Equipping:

The apostle *appointed elders* or pastors, who were entrusted with the nurturing of the disciples. Then he would go on to other places. The nature of his ministry made it necessary that he should be able at times to function as a pastor/elder (1 Peter 5:1; 2 John 1:1; 3 John 1:1). However, he never settled down anywhere to do the work of a permanent pastor or elder. Not only was he involved in recognizing and appointing elders, but also, if necessary, he would confront elders who were sinning (Acts 20:17-38, especially verses 31-32; 1 Timothy 3:1-7; 5:17-25; Titus 1:2-9).

Expanding:

The apostle gave priority time to *developing faithful "Timothys"* to whom he could *pass on* the Scriptures (2 Timothy 2:2). He was an extension agent or minister who was *responsible for planting and establishing the churches.*

The Church Planter's Instructions Given

Paul's Instruction:

The church planter's instructions are provided in Paul's letters to Timothy and Titus. They deal primarily with the church planter's life and ministry.

Godliness:

He is to *pay close attention to his own life and teaching and he is to train and discipline himself for the purpose of godliness.* His progress is evident to all. He is to work hard like a farmer, be disciplined as an athlete, and be untangled in civilian affairs as a soldier (1 Timothy 4:1-16; 2 Timothy 2:3-6; 1 Corinthians 9:24-27).

Preparedness:

Paul knew the roughness of the road, the hardness of the fight, the subtlety of the enemy, and the special dangers and temptations that beset the church planter; therefore, he had the need for constant vigilance and readiness.

The Church Planter's Authority

Authority:

The apostle's charge and authority comes from God. His work is to preach and teach in season and out (2 Timothy 4:1-5; Titus 2), to establish churches (Titus 1:5; Acts 14:23), to oversee churches and elders (1 Timothy 1:3; Titus 1:5; 1 Timothy 4:11-13; 5:1, 17, 19-20; 2 Timothy 4:2-5; Titus 2), to reprove, rebuke, exhort (1 Timothy 5:20-21; Titus 1:13-14; 2:15), guard against doctrines of demons and refute those who contradict their teaching (Titus 3:10-11; Acts 15:1-2; 1 Timothy 1:3-4) and to minister through prayer and faith (2 Timothy 4:1-4; 2:22-26; 1 Timothy 4:1-16). Their preparation, under the providential guidance of the Holy Spirit, is to study the Scriptures to obtain experiential knowledge by participating in the life and work of the local churches.

The Church Planter's Call Confirmed

Confirmation:

The apostle's call was received directly from the Lord and made known to the leaders by the Holy Spirit (Acts 13:2-4; 16:1-3). This is beautifully described in Acts 13:2, "While they were worshiping the Lord and fasting, the Holy Spirit said, 'Set apart for me Barnabas and Saul for the work to which I have called them'." The leader received from the Holy Spirit his calling confirmation (1 Timothy 4:1-4; 2 Timothy 1:6; Acts 13:2-3). He was to be available to minister locally and in other parts of the world as God would open and close doors. His call was primarily taking the gospel to new areas and establishing new and existing churches (Acts 13:1–14:26; 15:36–16:5; Philippians 1:3-7; 2:19-24; 1 Thessalonians 1:1-3: 3:13; 1 Timothy 3:14-16; Titus 1:5).

The Church Planter's Teamwork

Teams:

Apostles usually ministered in and with *"apostolic teams"*. These teams did not have authority over the local church elders, nor were they under the authority of the elders. Rather they were in complementary relationships. They functioned as part of the shepherding team, and alongside the elders when they resided in that local church for a period of time.

The apostles served as links among the existing churches and were also involved in starting and helping establish new churches. Several of the "other apostles" mentioned in the Scriptures were Andronicus, Apollos, Barnabas, Epaphras, Epaphroditus, Junias, Justus, Silas, Timothy, Titus, and Tychicus.

Mentoring:

There is a multiplying component— not only in seeing churches reproduce, but also in seeing their *teams reproduce*. God is still calling "wise master builders" to serve not only in planting and establishing the church but also in mentoring younger teams of church planters.

The Church Planter's Responsibilities

The *"kind of men they were"* provided a powerful validation of the truths they were teaching. They were men who were passionate about maintaining a clear conscience before both God and men (1 Thessalonians 1:5; 2:3, 10).

They *preached the gospel* to the unsaved and then established the disciples who had repented from their sins and believed (Acts 13:1-28; Colossians 2:7).

They served as a communication link *between the churches,* exchanging information and reports. They were itinerant laborers who traveled among the churches (Acts 14:27; 15:30-35; Colossians 4:7-8).

They *encouraged the hearts of the saints* through teaching, exhorting and admonishing them with the Word and by living among them as "living epistles" (1 Thessalonians 1:1-9).

They *"set in order what remained"* in newly founded churches by appointing elders and teaching them the whole counsel of God (Acts 20:25-38; Titus 1:5).

They *worked day and night with their own hands* to support their financial needs. In doing so they set an example for the saints that "it is more blessed to give than to receive". (Acts 20:35 NIV). Their working removed the possibility of people thinking they were being manipulated for the sake of financial gain by those proclaiming the gospel. They were in effect 'tent-makers' yet occasionally they were supported by churches, but not by a church where they were currently ministering. There were actual times when they even refused support (Acts 20:33-38; 1 Thessalonians 1:1-9; 2 Thessalonians 3).

Finally, they helped *resolve serious conflict* within the churches and confronted sin (Acts 15:1-41; Galatians 2:11-14; 2 Timothy 2:24-26).

Discussion Questions: Why are "apostles" and church planters often called pastors? _____

_____

_____

_____

What are the consequences if the role of "apostle" is neglected or confused with the role of Pastor?

_____

_____

_____

_____

_____

Church Planter's Financial Support

Tent-making Versus Full Support

To make tents or not to make tents? The question has relevance to church planters, not only because it is a biblical norm, but because more and more tent-makers today are seeing the advantage of working. One must realize that if church planters are receiving the bulk of their income from donor gifts, then they are forfeiting their ability to be an example to the majority of believers.

Paul, the Model Church Planter

Look at the model church planter, the Apostle Paul. He was the greatest church planter who ever lived, yet he deliberately chose to work with his hands to provide his own needs. With all his apostolic authority and connections with the churches Paul probably could have received full financial support, but he chose to support himself and his team companions. Paul's model of *working appears to have helped advance the gospel rather than hinder its progress as many believe today.*

Paul Showed Them (Acts 20:33-35)

Paul's example to the Ephesian elders is very clear: "I have not coveted anyone's silver or gold and clothing. You yourselves know that these hands of mine have supplied my own needs and the needs of my companions. In everything I did, *I showed you* that by this kind of hard work we must help the weak, remembering the words the Lord Jesus himself said, 'It is more blessed to give than to receive'." (Acts 20:33-35 NIV)

Paul Made Himself a Model (2 Thessalonians 3:7-13)

Another example was to the Thessalonians: "For you yourselves know how you ought to *follow our example*. We were not idle when we were with you, nor did we eat anyone's food without paying for it. On the contrary, we worked night and day, laboring and toiling so that we would not be a burden to any of you. We did this, not because we do not have the right to such help, but in order *to make ourselves a model for you to follow*. For even when we were with you, we gave you this rule: 'If a man will not work, he shall not eat.' We hear that some among you are idle. They are not busy; they are busybodies. Such people we command and urge in the Lord Jesus Christ to settle down and earn the bread they eat. And as for you brothers, never tire of doing what is right." (2 Thessalonians 3:7-13 NIV)

Paul Won the Respect of Outsiders (1 Thessalonians 4:11-12)

Even in Paul's first letter to the Thessalonians, he is concerned about his example: "Make it your ambition to lead a quiet life, to mind your own business and to work with your hands, just as we told you, so that your daily life may *win the respect of outsiders* and so that you will not be dependent on anybody" (1 Thessalonians 4:11-12 NIV).

Paul Gave Up His Right (1 Corinthians 9)

1 Corinthians chapter 9 contains one of the most direct discussions on the question of paid church planters found in the New Testament. Paul defends, with four arguments, his right as an apostle to be supported by those among whom he travels (verses 1-6). He argues from human experience (verse 7), the Old Testament agricultural law (verses 8-10; Deuteronomy 25:4), the practice of other workers (verses 11-12), and Old Testament Levitical custom (verse 13). But, Paul explicitly *gives up this right in order to minister more effectively* (verses 15-23) recognizing that the real reward is a spiritual inheritance yet to come (verses 24-27). Paul explains that he wants to make the gospel of Christ available without charge (verse 18).

Paul Wanted an Effective Ministry (2 Corinthians 7–12)

Paul did not want to be misunderstood or have the *effectiveness of his ministry reduced*. That is why Paul did not normally receive money from those he was presently ministering to (2 Corinthians 7:2-4; 11:20-21; 12:14-15, etc). He was willing to receive gifts after he had left, as in Philippi. Paul was willing to labor in accordance with God's provision, making tents or receiving support from others (Philippians 4:10-19). Regardless, Paul was content and free.

The Church Planter Norm

Those men who are completely financially supported need to realize that they have a limited ministry with respect to setting a good example for future leaders. The ideal model is the type of committed church planter who will serve as a model to all the members of the assemblies as he balances the responsibilities of family, job, and ministry. The *self-supporting church planter should be the norm* in a reproducing model of church life, although he is free to receive support or work.

Who Will Be That One Man?

It is almost universally taken for granted that credible missionary work is the work of a *paid professional who trains up indigenous leaders who think they must be fully supported.* Westerners have carried this philosophy all over the world as if it were an essential part of the gospel. The expansion of the church, reduced to its elements, is a very simple thing. It asks for no elaborate organization, no large finances, and no great numbers of paid missionaries. In its new beginning it may be the work of one man who is neither learned in things of this world nor rich in the wealth of this world. Rather, it is one who has been with Jesus and is full of the Holy Spirit!

Discussion Questions: Did Paul's work or tentmaking trade enhance and accelerate his ministry or did it hinder or inhibit his ministry? _____

_____

_____

_____

_____

Support your answer from the Scriptures. _____

_____

_____

_____

_____

_____

_____

Lesson 40
The Role of Pastors/Elders/Bishops/Overseers

The Word of God uses these words or terms interchangeably for the same function which is to shepherd and oversee the flock or the household of God. These words are always used in the plural indicating that the norm was always more than one. They are shepherds under Christ the Great Shepherd and their qualifications and authority to rule the church come from the Word of God. *(Note: At the end of this lesson there is an evaluation of pastors/elders/bishops character qualifications.)*

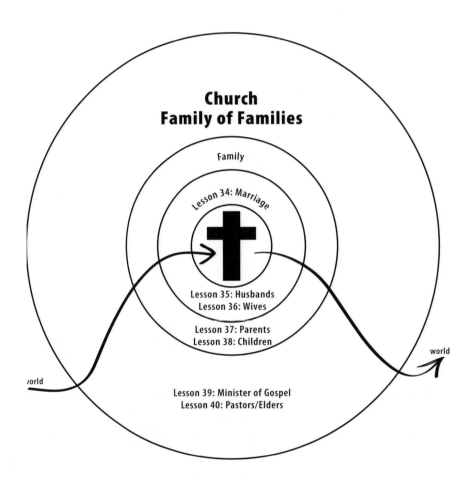

Observation: Read and observe the following verses and write down what you learn about the role of Pastors/Elders/Bishops/Overseers.

Example: 1 Timothy 3:14-15 _Paul writes to Timothy on how <u>one ought to behave</u> in the <u>household</u>_ _of God,</u> which is the <u>church of the living God,</u> a pillar and buttress of truth._

Titus 1:5 _____

_____

Acts 20:17-38 _____

_____

1 Timothy 3:1-7 _____

_____

1 Timothy 5:17-20 _____

_____

Titus 1:5-9 _____

_____

Hebrews 13:7 _____

_____

1 Peter 5:1-4 _____

_____

Respond: Based on these verses, write a brief summary of the key principles and functions that you observed from God's Word that every person, family and church could follow at any time, in any culture. (Absolutes) _____

_____

_____

Discussion: Contrast these principles with your life, family and church experience today.

_____

_____

_____

What changes do you need to make in your life, family and church here and now? _____

_____

_____

Application: How and when will you make these changes in your life, family and church?

_____

_____

_____

Qualifications for Pastors/Elders/Bishops Assessment

The following qualifications should be evaluated at least every year independently, with your wife and with the other leaders in your church or ministry. Although no one is perfect in every area, there should be steady progress in your character satisfaction. Circle the number that expresses your assessment below

As to God and His Word

Not a new convert (1 Timothy 3:6). Do you truly know the Lord and are you in a continual progress in spiritual maturity and growth?

Dissatisfied   1   2   3   4   5   6   7   Satisfied

Devout (Titus 1:8). Do you demonstrate a definite commitment to know, love, and walk with God?

Dissatisfied   1   2   3   4   5   6   7   Satisfied

Holding fast to the faithful Word . . . able to exhort . . . and refute . . . (1 Timothy 3:2; Titus 1:9). Do you have that quality of life and biblical knowledge that enables you to communicate the Word of God to others effectively maintaining a gentle attitude?

Dissatisfied   1   2   3   4   5   6   7   Satisfied

As to Himself

If a man aspires to the office of overseer (1 Timothy 3:1). Do you have a compelling desire to serve the Lord and the body of Christ as an overseer of the flock, not under compulsion but voluntarily?

Dissatisfied   1   2   3   4   5   6   7   Satisfied

Temperate (1 Timothy 3:2). In daily life, do you tend to react under the Spirit's control according to biblical principles?

Dissatisfied   1   2   3   4   5   6   7   Satisfied

Prudent (1 Timothy 3:2). Do you have a correct view of yourself in relationship to God and other Christians?

Dissatisfied   1   2   3   4   5   6   7   Satisfied

Not quick tempered (Titus 1:7). Do you have a short fuse? Do you harbor feelings of resentment over a period of time?

Dissatisfied   1   2   3   4   5   6   7   Satisfied

As to His Family

Husband of one wife (1 Timothy 3:2; Titus 1:6). How is your relationship with your wife? Literally, are you a one-woman man?

Dissatisfied   1   2   3   4   5   6   7   Satisfied

One who manages his own household well (1 Timothy 3:4-5; Titus 1:6). Do your wife and children love, respect, and follow your leadership and are they responding to your God and His claim on their lives?

Dissatisfied   1   2   3   4   5   6   7   Satisfied

As to Others

Hospitable (1 Timothy 3:2; Titus 1:8). Literally, are you "a lover of strangers" and do you use your home as a means to minister to others?

Dissatisfied   1   2   3   4   5   6   7   Satisfied

Able to teach (1 Timothy 3:2). Are you able to communicate the Word of God to others and handle those who disagree with you in a patient and gentle manner? Do others recognize your ability to teach and communicate the Word?

Dissatisfied   1   2   3   4   5   6   7   Satisfied

Not self-willed (Titus 1:7). Do you always have to have your own way or do you set aside your own preferences in order to promote unity and care for the needs of others?

Dissatisfied   1   2   3   4   5   6   7   Satisfied

Loving what is good (Titus 1:8). Do you desire to associate yourself with truth, honor, and integrity; and do you take advantage of opportunities to do good to all men in order to build them up rather than tear them down?

Dissatisfied   1   2   3   4   5   6   7   Satisfied

Not pugnacious or a striker, i.e., anger out of control (1 Timothy 3:3; Titus 1:7). Do you show a tendency to be either physically or verbally abusive because of angry feelings?

Dissatisfied   1   2   3   4   5   6   7   Satisfied

Contentious (1 Timothy 3:3). Do you purposely take the opposite point of view from others for self-seeking reasons such as jealousy or selfish ambition?

Dissatisfied   1   2   3   4   5   6   7   Satisfied

Gentle (1 Timothy 3:3). Are you yielding, showing gentleness and kindness, or are you heavy-handed, insisting on the letter of the law?

Dissatisfied   1   2   3   4   5   6   7   Satisfied

Just (Titus 1:8). Are you able to make just decisions, those that are wise, fair, impartial, objective, and honest according to Scripture?

Dissatisfied   1   2   3   4   5   6   7   Satisfied

Respectable, orderly, balanced (1 Timothy 3:2). Are you respected by others because your life adorns the Word of God in a blended and balanced manner?

Dissatisfied   1   2   3   4   5   6   7   Satisfied

Having a good reputation with those on the outside (1 Timothy 1:7). Do you have a good reputation among unbelievers because you have a lifestyle of unquestioned integrity?

Dissatisfied   1   2   3   4   5   6   7   Satisfied

As to Things

Free from the love of money (1 Timothy 3:3; Titus 1:7). Do you seek significance, security, and primary satisfaction from material wealth? Do you seek His kingdom and His righteousness first?

Dissatisfied   1   2   3   4   5   6   7   Satisfied

Not addicted to wine (1 Timothy 3:3; Titus 1:7). Are you free from any kind of addiction which might take control of your life or cause weaker Christians to stumble (Romans 14:13-21)?

Dissatisfied   1   2   3   4   5   6   7   Satisfied

Discuss: Why did you think people use pastors, elders and bishops for different titles and functions when biblically they are used interchangeably and mean the same thing? _____

_____

_____

Why is academic and social standing used more as a qualification than character? _____

_____

_____

_____

What can you do to promote the usage of the true biblical role and function of elders? _____

_____

_____

_____

_____

Lesson 41
The Role of Deacons

The Word of God defines the role and function of deacons as servants who are involved in the cultural, temporal and material service of the church under the rule of the elders. Since their service reflects the elders who reflect Christ, deacons need to be qualified according to the Word of God. *(Note: At the end of this lesson there is an evaluation of the deacon's character qualifications.)*

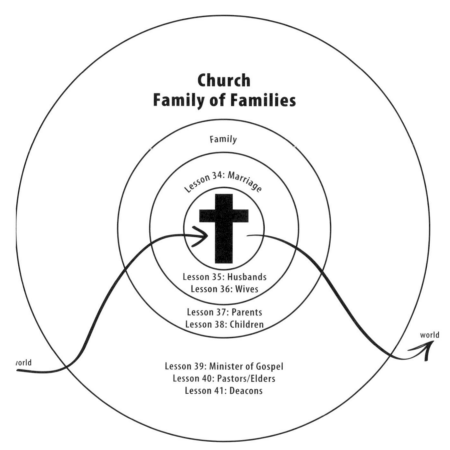

**Church
Family of Families**

Family

Lesson 34: Marriage

Lesson 35: Husbands
Lesson 36: Wives

Lesson 37: Parents
Lesson 38: Children

Lesson 39: Minister of Gospel
Lesson 40: Pastors/Elders
Lesson 41: Deacons

world

world

Observation: Read and observe the following verses and write down what you learn about the role of Deacons.

Example: 1 Timothy 3:14-15 <u>Paul writes to Timothy on how one ought to behave in the household of God, which is the church of the living God,</u> a pillar and buttress of truth.

Acts 6:1-7 _____

_____

_____

Romans 16:1 _____

_____

_____

1 Timothy 3:8-13 _____

_____

_____

Titus 1:5 _____

_____

_____

Respond: Based on these verses, write a brief summary of the key principles and functions that you observed from God's Word that every person, family and church could follow at any time, in any culture. (Absolutes) _____

_____

_____

Discussion: Contrast these principles with your life, family and church experience today.

_____

_____

_____

What changes do you need to make in your life, family and church here and now? _____

_____

_____

_____

Application: How and when will you make these changes in your life, family and church?

_____

_____

_____

_____

Qualifications for Deacons Assessment

The following qualifications should be evaluated at least every year independently, with your wife and with the other leaders in your church or ministry. Although no one is perfect in every area, there should be steady progress in your character satisfaction. Circle the number that expresses your assessment below:

In General

Tested . . . beyond reproach (1 Timothy 3:10). Having been observed over a period of time, are there any violations in the qualities needed to serve that would disqualify you as a deacon, or do you need more time?

Dissatisfied   1   2   3   4   5   6   7   Satisfied

As to God and His Word

Holding to the mystery of the faith with a clear conscience (1 Timothy 3:8) "The mystery of the faith" refers to the body of Christian doctrine with a clear conscience. Do you keep a clear conscience before God?

Dissatisfied   1   2   3   4   5   6   7   Satisfied

As to Self

Men of dignity (1 Timothy 3:8). Do you take your life and work seriously as a part of your devotion to the Lord?

Dissatisfied   1   2   3   4   5   6   7   Satisfied

Not double tongued (1 Timothy 3:8). Are you hypocritical, saying one thing to one person and something contradictory to another?

Dissatisfied   1   2   3   4   5   6   7   Satisfied

As to Things

Not addicted to much wine (1 Timothy 3:8). Are you addicted to anything that is controlling your life or causing a weaker Christian to stumble and sin against God?

Dissatisfied   1   2   3   4   5   6   7   Satisfied

Not fond of sordid gain (1 Timothy 3:8). Are you controlled by the desire for material wealth or do you seek His kingdom and righteousness first?

Dissatisfied   1   2   3   4   5   6   7   Satisfied

As to Family

A husband of one wife (1 Timothy 3:12). Are you a one-woman man? Do you have a good relationship with your wife?

Dissatisfied   1   2   3   4   5   6   7   Satisfied

Good managers of their children and their own households (1 Timothy 3:12). Do your wife and children love, respect, and follow your leadership? Are they responding to God and His claim on their lives?

Dissatisfied   1   2   3   4   5   6   7   Satisfied

Discuss: What are the differences between Deacons and Elders? _____

_____

_____

_____

_____

Why are deacons sometimes in the position of eldership and leadership? _____

_____

_____

_____

_____

Why are the qualifications for a deacon so rigid? _____

_____

_____

_____

_____

Lesson 42
The Role of Older Men

The Word of God supports the important role of older men in the early church and exhorts them to live a life of self-control, sound faith and steadfastness. They also have a very important function in teaching younger men by word and example. In the Old Testament older men were referred to as elders and were to be respected for their wisdom.

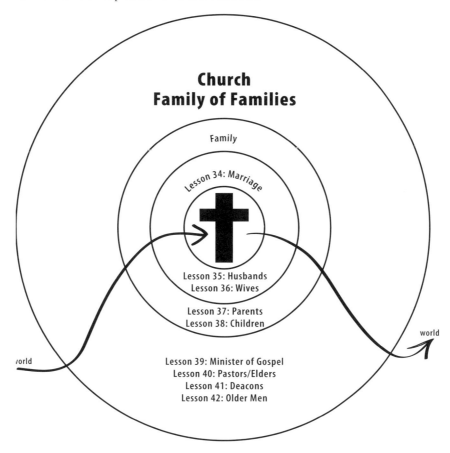

Church Family of Families

Family

Lesson 34: Marriage

Lesson 35: Husbands
Lesson 36: Wives

Lesson 37: Parents
Lesson 38: Children

Lesson 39: Minister of Gospel
Lesson 40: Pastors/Elders
Lesson 41: Deacons
Lesson 42: Older Men

world

world

Observation: Read and observe the following verses and write down what you learn about the role of older men.

Example: 1 Timothy 3:14-15 _Paul writes to Timothy on how one ought to behave in the household of God, which is the church of the living God, a pillar and buttress of truth._

Psalm 148:12-13 _____

_____

_____

Proverbs 20:27-29 _____

_____

Acts 2:17 _____

_____

1 Timothy 5:1 _____

_____

Titus 1:5 _____

_____

Titus 2:1-2 _____

_____

Titus 3:8-11 _____

_____

1 Peter 5:1-5 _____

_____

Respond: Based on these verses, write a brief summary of the key principles and functions that you observed from God's Word that every person, family and church could follow at any time, in any culture. (Absolutes) _____

_____

_____

Discussion: Contrast these principles with your life, family and church experience today.

_____

_____

What changes do you need to make in your life, family and church here and now? _____

_____

_____

Application: How and when will you make these changes in your life, family and church?

_____

_____

_____

_____

Lesson 43
The Role of Older Women

The Word of God clearly supports the important role of women in the early church especially in their service for Christ, Paul, and the apostles. They also have a very important role in teaching younger women by word and example. Some of these women were probably widows who were serving as deaconesses which enabled them to be more devoted to serving.

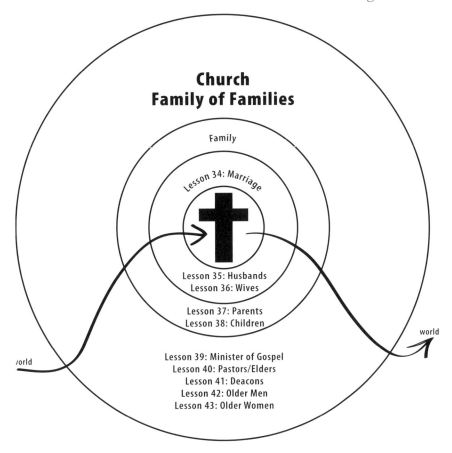

Observation: Read and observe the following verses and write down what you learn about the role of older women.

Example: 1 Timothy 3:14-15 _Paul writes to Timothy on how one ought to behave in the household of God, which is the church of the living God, a pillar and buttress of truth._

1 Timothy 5:1-2 _____

_____

_____

Titus 1:5 _____

_____

_____

Titus 2:3-5 _____

_____

_____

Respond: Based on these verses, write a brief summary of the key principles and functions that you observed from God's Word that every person, family and church could follow at any time, in any culture. (Absolutes) _____

_____

_____

_____

Discussion: Contrast these principles with your life, family and church experience today.

_____

_____

_____

_____

What changes do you need to make in your life, family and church here and now? _____

_____

_____

_____

Application: How and when will you make these changes in your life, family and church?

_____

_____

_____

_____

Lesson 44
The Role of Younger Men

The Word of God clearly defines the role and responsibility of young men in the family of God. Today many young men are not serving and older men are retiring from service, but God declares they both have very important roles and functions within the church; younger men are to learn from older men.

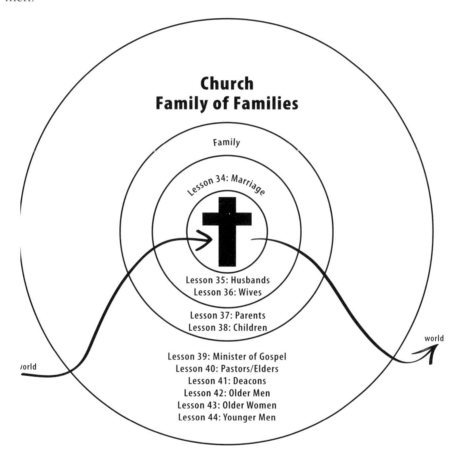

Observation: Read and observe the following verses and write down what you learn about the role of younger men.

Example: 1 Timothy 3:14-15 _Paul writes to Timothy on how one ought to behave in the household of God, which is the church of the living God, a pillar and buttress of truth._

Psalm 119:9-16 _____

_____

_____

Proverbs 20:27-29 _____

_____

Acts 2:17 _____

_____

1 Timothy 5:1 _____

_____

Titus 1:5 _____

_____

Titus 2:1-7 _____

_____

1 Peter 5:5 _____

_____

Respond: Based on these verses, write a brief summary of the key principles and functions that you observed from God's Word that every person, family and church could follow at any time, in any culture. (Absolutes) _____

_____

_____

Discussion: Contrast these principles with your life, family and church experience today.

_____

_____

_____

What changes do you need to make in your life, family and church here and now? _____

_____

_____

_____

Application: How and when will you make these changes in your life, family and church?

_____

_____

_____

_____

Lesson 45
The Role of Younger Women

The Word of God clearly defines the role and responsibility of young women in the family of God. Today many young women are leaving the church and older women are retiring from service, but God declares they both have very important roles and functions within the Body of Christ. Younger women are to learn from older women so they can become mature wives and mothers.

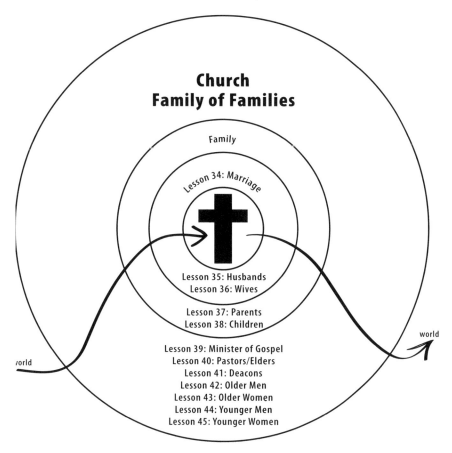

Church Family of Families

Family

Lesson 34: Marriage

Lesson 35: Husbands
Lesson 36: Wives

Lesson 37: Parents
Lesson 38: Children

Lesson 39: Minister of Gospel
Lesson 40: Pastors/Elders
Lesson 41: Deacons
Lesson 42: Older Men
Lesson 43: Older Women
Lesson 44: Younger Men
Lesson 45: Younger Women

world

world

Observation: Read and observe the following verses and write down what you learn about the role of younger women.

Example: 1 Timothy 3:14-15 <u>Paul writes to Timothy on how <u>one ought to behave</u> in the <u>household of God,</u> which is the <u>church of the living God,</u> a pillar and buttress of truth.</u>

Psalm 119:9-6 _____

_____

_____

1 Timothy 5:1-2 _____

_____

_____

Titus 1:5 _____

_____

_____

Titus 2:1-5 _____

_____

_____

Respond: Based on these verses, write a brief summary of the key principles and functions that you observed from God's Word that every person, family and church could follow at any time, in any culture. (Absolutes) _____

_____

_____

_____

Discussion: Contrast these principles with your life, family and church experience today.

_____

_____

_____

_____

What changes do you need to make in your life, family and church here and now? _____

_____

_____

_____

Application: How and when will you make these changes in your life, family and church?

_____

_____

_____

_____

Biblical Roles in the Church Family

Lesson 46
The Role of Widows

I learned more from the Word of God about widows than any other role. Their role and function is tremendously important to the household of God. I believe they were probably deaconesses or servants in the early church, involved in serving the apostles and elders. Their qualifications and responsibilities are very important to the church as you will learn from the Word of God.

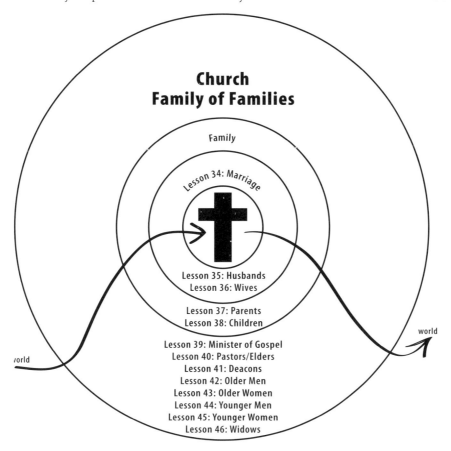

Church Family of Families

Family

Lesson 34: Marriage

Lesson 35: Husbands
Lesson 36: Wives

Lesson 37: Parents
Lesson 38: Children

Lesson 39: Minister of Gospel
Lesson 40: Pastors/Elders
Lesson 41: Deacons
Lesson 42: Older Men
Lesson 43: Older Women
Lesson 44: Younger Men
Lesson 45: Younger Women
Lesson 46: Widows

world

world

Observation: Read and observe the following verses and write down what you learn about the role of widows.

Example: 1 Timothy 3:14-15 <u>Paul writes to Timothy on how <u>one ought to behave</u> in the <u>household</u> of God,</u> which is the <u>church of the living God,</u> a pillar and buttress of truth.

Luke 21:1-4 _____

_____

_____

Acts 6:1 _____

_____

_____

1 Corinthians 7:39-40 _____

_____

_____

1 Timothy 5:1-16 _____

_____

_____

Titus 1:5 _____

_____

_____

Respond: Based on these verses, write a brief summary of the key principles and functions that you observed from God's Word that every person, family and church could follow at any time, in any culture. (Absolutes) _____

_____

_____

Discussion: Contrast these principles with your life, family and church experience today.

_____

_____

_____

_____

What changes do you need to make in your life, family and church here and now? _____

_____

_____

_____

Application: How and when will you make these changes in your life, family and church?

_____

_____

_____

_____

Project K
Setting the Church in Order

1. Make an outline or diagram or chart of Paul's concept of managing the church using the different roles and responsibilities within the family of families.

Ministers of the Gospel: _____

_____

_____

Pastors/Elders: _____

_____

_____

Deacons: _____

_____

_____

Older Men: _____

_____

_____

Older Women: _____

_____

_____

Younger Men: _____

_____

_____

Younger Women: _____

_____

_____

Widows: _____

_____

_____

2. Compare your church with your outline or diagram (above). Where does your church need to change? _____

_____

_____

_____

_____

_____

3. What can you do to help make that happen? _____

_____

_____

_____

_____

_____

_____

4. Write a brief strategy of your role and responsibility in your church family.

_____

_____

_____

_____

_____

_____

_____

Biblical Issues in the Church, the Family of Families

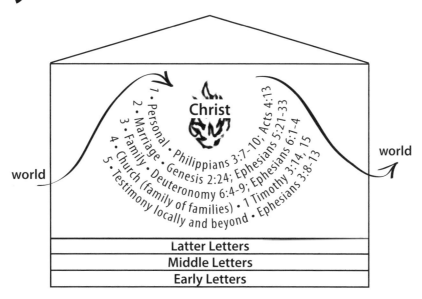

Now we transition from the roles in the household to issues that the family and family of families face. The solution to every issue that you and the church will face is found in God's Word. Under the control of the Holy Spirit and the Authority of God's Word, these lessons will help you and the leaders resolve many inevitable problems in the church. As a review, try to fill in the blanks in the diagram below without looking back:

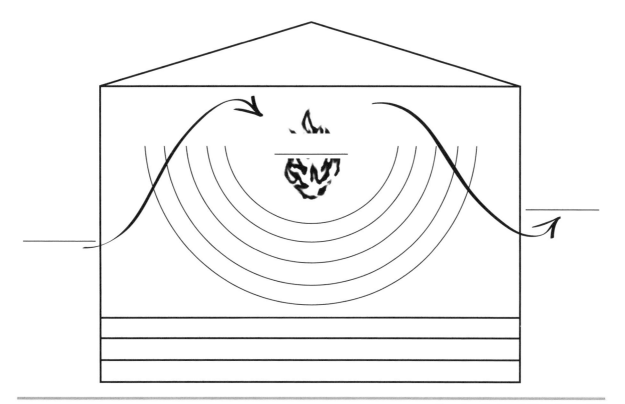

Biblical Issues in the Church Family

Lesson 47
Authority and Sufficiency of God's Word

The Word of God or "Scripture alone" is your foundation. Building on anything else is doomed for collapse sooner or later. As you hear God speak concerning His own Word, you will observe that the living Word of God is enough and provides you with *everything* you need to fulfill your calling.

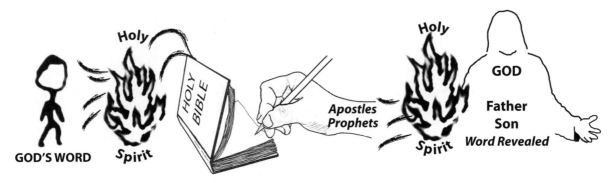

Observation: Read and observe the following verses and write down what you learn about the authority and sufficiency of God's Word in His household, family and church.

Example: 1 Timothy 3:14-15 _Paul writes to Timothy on how <u>one ought to behave</u> in the <u>household</u> <u>of God,</u> which is the <u>church of the living God,</u> a pillar and buttress of truth._

Psalm 19:7-14 _____

_____

_____

Psalm 119:9-16 _____

_____

_____

Psalm 138:2 _____

_____

_____

Jeremiah 23:28-29 _____

_____

_____

John 1:1, 14 _____

_____

_____

Acts 6:7 _____

_____

_____

Acts 12:24 _____

_____

_____

Acts 13:49 _____

_____

_____

Acts 19:20 _____

_____

_____

2 Thessalonians 2:13 _____

_____

_____

2 Timothy 3:16-17 _____

_____

_____

Hebrews 4:12 _____

_____

_____

1 Peter 1:22-25 _____

_____

_____

2 Peter 1:3-4 _____

_____

_____

2 Peter 1:19-21 _____

_____

_____

Respond: Based on these verses, write a brief summary of the key principles and functions that you observed from God's Word that every person, family and church could follow at any time, in any culture. (Absolutes) _____

_____

_____

_____

Discussion: Contrast these principles with your life, family and church experience today.

_____

_____

_____

_____

What changes do you need to make in your life, family and church here and now? _____

_____

_____

_____

Application: How and when will you make these changes in your life, family and church?

_____

_____

_____

_____

Biblical Issues in the Church Family

Lesson 48
Hearing from God—Quiet Time

The Word of God teaches that spending time daily with God is absolutely vital to your spiritual life and walk in Christ. When you spend time alone with the Lord, you are in contact with what matters most. The most important thing we can do is something we all can do; spend time with Christ in the Word and in prayer which is a joyful privilege.

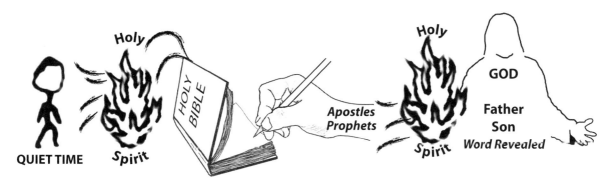

Observation: Read and observe the following verses and write down what you learn as a result of hearing from God and/or quiet time with God.

Example: 1 Timothy 3:14-15 _Paul writes to Timothy on how <u>one ought to behave</u> in the <u>household of God,</u> which is the <u>church of the living God,</u> a pillar and buttress of truth._

Joshua 1:8 _____

_____

Psalm 5:3 _____

_____

Jeremiah 15:16 _____

_____

Matthew 4:4 _____

_____

Matthew 6:6 _____

_____

Matthew 6:11 _____

_____

Mark 1:35 _____

_____

John 6:25-51 and Exodus 16:13-21 _____

_____

Acts 4:13 _____

_____

Hebrews 5:11–6:1 _____

_____

1Peter 1:22–2:3 _____

_____

Respond: Based on these verses, write a brief summary of the key principles and functions that you observed from God's Word that every person, family and church could follow at any time, in any culture. (Absolutes) _____

_____

_____

Discussion: Contrast these principles with your life, family and church experience today.

_____

_____

_____

What changes do you need to make in your life, family and church here and now? _____

_____

_____

Application: How and when will you make these changes in your life, family and church?

_____

_____

_____

Biblical Issues in the Church Family

Lesson 49
Servant Leaders

Servant leadership is a foreign concept in the church today. In many instances, the humblest of all faiths over the years degenerated into a power hungry and self-seeking organization, competing for bigger and better. Now hear God speak and learn what true servant leadership means.

Observation: Read and observe the following verses and write down what you learn about servant leadership.

1 Timothy 3:14-15 ___Paul writes to Timothy on how <u>one ought to behave</u> in the <u>household of God,</u>___
<u>which is the <u>church of the living God,</u> a pillar and buttress of truth.___

John 3:30 _____

_____

Matthew 11:29 _____

_____

Matthew 20:20-28 _____

_____

Matthew 23:1-12 _____

_____

Mark 9:33-35 _____

_____

Mark 10:35-45 _____

_____

Luke 22:24-27 _____

_____

John 13:12-15 _____

_____

1 Thessalonians 2:2-12 _____

_____

I Corinthians 1:26-31 _____

_____

Philippians 2:3-11 _____

_____

1 Peter 5:5-6 _____

_____

Respond: Based on these verses, write a brief summary of the key principles and functions that you observed from God's Word that every person, family and church could follow at any time, in any culture. (Absolutes) _____

_____

_____

Discussion: Contrast these principles with your life, family and church experience today.

_____

_____

_____

What changes do you need to make in your life, family and church here and now? _____

_____

_____

Application: How and when will you make these changes in your life, family and church?

_____

_____

_____

Lesson 50
The Baptism of the Holy Spirit

Much of life and ministry that is going on in the church today is pre-Pentecostal. We teach about the incarnation, death, burial and resurrection of Christ but neglect the ascension and Pentecost. Without Pentecost there is no hope, no resurrection power, no transformation and no significant witness. Having the Holy Spirit in us is better than having Christ with us!

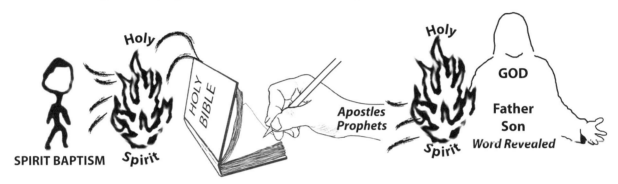

Observation: Read and observe the following verses and write down what you learn about the Holy Spirit.

Example: 1 Timothy 3:14-15 _Paul writes to Timothy on how <u>one ought to behave</u> in the <u>household</u> of God,_ which is the <u>church of the living God,</u> a pillar and buttress of truth.

Genesis 1:1-2 _____

_____

_____

2 Kings 6:13-18 _____

_____

_____

Ezekiel 36:25–37:14 _____

_____

John 1:32-33 _____

_____

John 3:3-8 _____

_____

John 7:37-39 _____

_____

_____

John 14:12-26 _____

_____

_____

John 16:7-14 _____

_____

_____

Acts 1:8 _____

_____

_____

Acts 2:1-47 _____

_____

_____

1 Corinthians 12:12-13 _____

_____

_____

Ephesians 1:13-20 _____

_____

_____

Ephesians 3:20 _____

_____

_____

Romans 8:1-11 _____

_____

_____

Galatians 3:2 _____

_____

_____

Galatians 5:16-25 _____

_____

Ephesians 4:30-31 _____

_____

Ephesians 5:18 _____

_____

Acts 5:32 _____

_____

Acts 7:51 _____

_____

1 Thessalonians 5:19 _____

_____

Respond: Based on these verses, write a brief summary of the key principles and functions that you observed from God's Word that every person, family and church could follow at any time, in any culture. (Absolutes) _____

_____

_____

Discussion: Contrast these principles with your life, family and church experience today.

_____

_____

What changes do you need to make in your life, family and church here and now? _____

_____

_____

_____

Application: How and when will you make these changes in your life, family and church?

_____

_____

_____

_____

Lesson 51
Water Baptism

Baptism is an outward rite instituted by Christ to be administered by the church. It shows a visual picture of one's spiritual baptism at the time of salvation. Baptism is an act of obedience to the Lord's command and no special grace is granted although obedience to this command is evident of one's growth in the grace and knowledge of the Lord Jesus Christ.

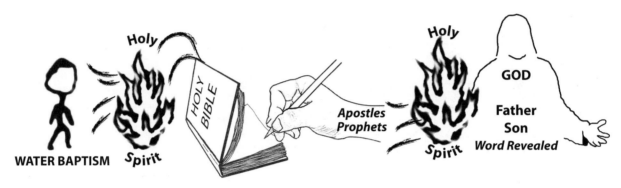

Observation: Read and observe the following verses and write down what you learn about water baptism.

Example: 1 Timothy 3:14-15 <u>Paul writes to Timothy on how <u>one ought to behave</u> in the <u>household of God,</u> which is the <u>church of the living God,</u> a pillar and buttress of truth.</u>

Matthew 3:13-17 _____

_____

Matthew 10:32-33 _____

_____

Matthew 28:19-20 _____

_____

Mark 1:9-10 _____

_____

Luke 3:1-22 _____

_____

John 3:23 _____

_____

Acts 2:41 _____

_____

Acts 8:12-13 _____

_____

Acts 8:36-39 _____

_____

Acts 16:31-34 _____

_____

Acts 18:8 _____

_____

Respond: Based on these verses, write a brief summary of the key principles and functions that you observed from God's Word that every person, family and church could follow at any time, in any culture. (Absolutes) _____

_____

_____

_____

Discussion: Contrast these principles with your life, family and church experience today.

_____

_____

_____

What changes do you need to make in your life, family and church here and now? _____

_____

_____

_____

Application: How and when will you make these changes in your life, family and church?

_____

_____

_____

_____

Lesson 52
Serving One Another (Church Membership)

Churches today, in an attempt to control and measure their successes, have devised a worldly membership method which is foreign to the Bible. As you hear from God's Word, you will observe a membership based on each person's commitment to one another in the Body of Christ, under the direction of the Holy Spirit.

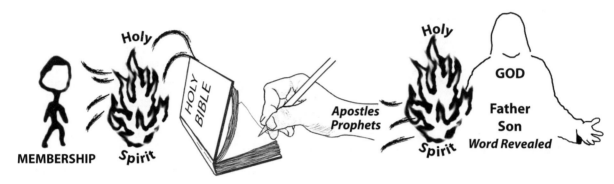

Observation: Read and observe the following verses and write down what you learn about church membership.

Example: 1 Timothy 3:14-15 _Paul writes to Timothy on how one ought to behave in the household of God, which is the church of the living God, a pillar and buttress of truth._

Galatians 5:13 _____

_____

Galatians 6:2 _____

_____

1 Thessalonians 4:18–5:11 _____

_____

Romans 12:5-10 _____

_____

Romans 13:8 _____

_____

Romans 15:5-14 _____

_____

Ephesians 4:2 _____

_____

Ephesians 5:21 _____

_____

Philippians 2:3-4 _____

_____

Colossians 3:12-14 _____

_____

James 5:16 _____

_____

1 Peter 5:5 _____

_____

Respond: Based on these verses, write a brief summary of the key principles and functions that you observed from God's Word that every person, family and church could follow at any time, in any culture. (Absolutes) _____

_____

_____

Discussion: Contrast these principles with your life, family and church experience today.

_____

_____

_____

What changes do you need to make in your life, family and church here and now? _____

_____

_____

Application: How and when will you make these changes in your life, family and church?

_____

_____

_____

Biblical Issues in the Church Family

Lesson 53
Handling Conflict

The lack of power and impact on today's churches can be directly contributed to their failure to address conflict and sin in the church, the Bride of Christ. Following the Scriptures on handling conflict can reestablish power, unity, purity, restoration and testimony within the Body of Christ for His glory. (Note: See Chart at end of this lesson for help in handling conflict.)

Observation: Read and observe the following verses and write down what you learn about handling conflict.

Example: 1 Timothy 3:14-15 _Paul writes to Timothy on how <u>one ought to behave</u> in the <u>household of God,</u> which is the <u>church of the living God,</u> a pillar and buttress of truth._

Matthew 18:15-18 _____

_____

Acts 15:1-41 _____

_____

Galatians 2:1-14 _____

_____

Galatians 5:12-6:5 _____

_____

2 Thessalonians 3:5-16 _____

_____

1 Corinthians 5:1-6:11 _____

_____

2 Corinthians 2:1-14; 7:5-13 _____

_____

Philippians 4:2-7 _____

_____

1 Timothy 5:19-22 _____

_____

Titus 1:9-16 _____

_____

Titus 3:9-11 _____   _____

_____

2 Timothy 2:14-16 _____

_____

Respond: Based on these verses, write a brief summary of the key principles and functions that you observed from God's Word that every person, family and church could follow at any time, in any culture. (Absolutes) _____

_____

Discussion: Contrast these principles with your life, family and church experience today.

_____

_____

_____

What changes do you need to make in your life, family and church here and now? _____

_____

_____

Application: How and when will you make these changes in your life, family and church?

_____

_____

_____

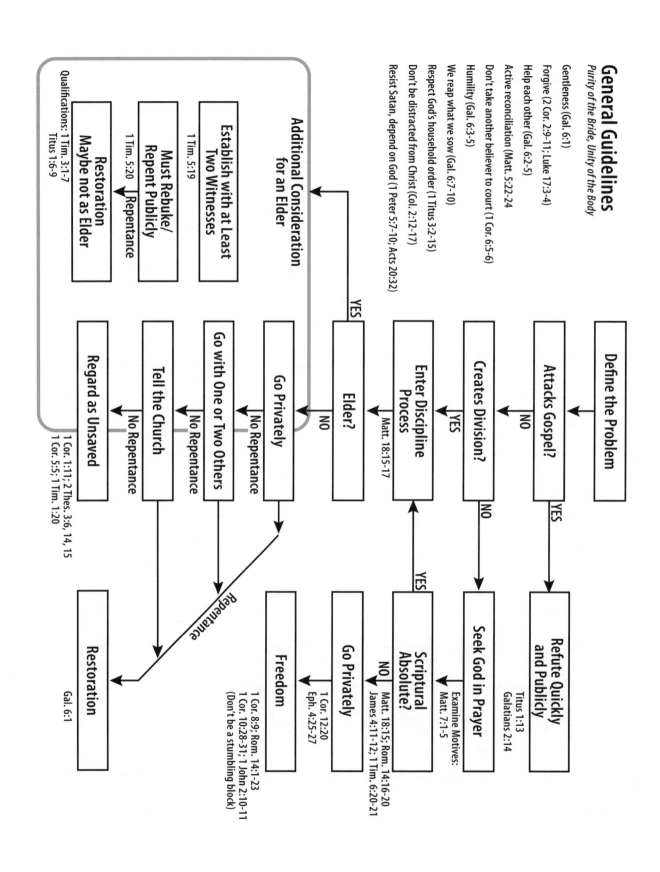

General Guidelines
Purity of the Bride, Unity of the Body

Gentleness (Gal. 6:1)
Forgive (2 Cor. 2:9-11; Luke 17:3-4)
Help each other (Gal. 6:2-5)
Active reconciliation (Matt. 5:22-24)
Don't take another believer to court (1 Cor. 6:5-6)
Humility (Gal. 6:3-5)
We reap what we sow (Gal. 6:7-10)
Respect God's household order (1 Titus 3:2-15)
Don't be distracted from Christ (Col. 2:12-17)
Resist Satan, depend on God (1 Peter 5:7-10; Acts 20:32)

Define the Problem

Attacks Gospel? — YES → **Refute Quickly and Publicly** (Titus 1:13, Galatians 2:14)
NO →

Creates Division? — YES → **Seek God in Prayer** (Examine Motives: Matt. 7:1-5)
NO →

Enter Discipline Process (Matt. 18:15-17)

Scriptural Absolute? — YES; NO → **Go Privately** (1 Cor. 12:20, Eph. 4:25-27) → **Freedom** (1 Cor. 8:9; Rom. 14:1-23; 1 Cor. 10:28-31; 1 John 2:10-11; Don't be a stumbling block)
NO: Matt. 18:15; Rom. 14:16-20; James 4:11-12; 1 Tim. 6:20-21

Elder? — YES → **Additional Consideration for an Elder**; NO →

Go Privately — No Repentance → **Go with One or Two Others** — No Repentance → **Tell the Church** — No Repentance → **Regard as Unsaved** (1 Cor. 1:11; 2 Thes. 3:6, 14, 15; 1 Cor. 5:5; 1 Tim. 1:20)

Repentance → **Restoration** (Gal. 6:1)

Additional Consideration for an Elder

Establish with at Least Two Witnesses (1 Tim. 5:19)

Must Rebuke/Repent Publicly (1 Tim. 5:20) — Repentance →

Restoration Maybe not as Elder
Qualifications: 1 Tim. 3:1-7; Titus 1:6-9

Adapted from Managing Conflict in the Church Chart by Glenn Vonk.

Lesson 54

Assembly Meetings

The life of our meetings and gatherings in the family of Christ has been stifled by man-made traditions and dead forms for way too long. As you read God's Word, you will learn how little biblical basis exists for what we do in our assembly meetings today. In the early church, Christ was clearly the head of their meetings and all family members were free to participate under the direction of the Holy Spirit.

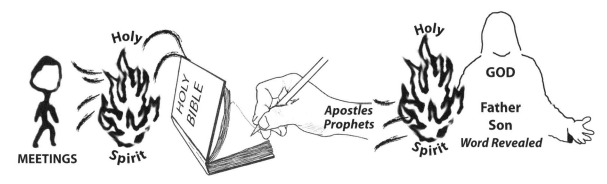

Observation: Read and observe the following verses and write down what you learn about assembly meetings.

Example: 1 Timothy 3:14-15 Paul writes to Timothy on how <u>one ought to behave</u> in the <u>household of God,</u> which is the <u>church of the living God,</u> a pillar and buttress of truth.

Acts 2:42-47 _____

_____

Acts 11:19-26 _____

_____

Acts 19:8-10 _____

_____

Acts 20:7-12 _____

_____

1 Corinthians 11:17–14:40 _____

_____

Romans 16:5 _____

_____

Ephesians 5:15-21 _____

_____

Colossians 1:18 _____

_____

1 Timothy 2:1-15 _____

_____

1 Timothy 4:6-16 _____

_____

Respond: Based on these verses, write a brief summary of the key principles and functions that you observed from God's Word that every person, family and church could follow at any time, in any culture. (Absolutes) _____

_____

_____

Discussion: Contrast these principles with your life, family and church experience today.

_____

_____

_____

What changes do you need to make in your life, family and church here and now? _____

_____

_____

_____

Application: How and when will you make these changes in your life, family and church?

_____

_____

_____

_____

Lesson 55
Lord's Supper

Tradition and routine have sucked the life and heart out of the celebration of the Lord's Supper. In this memorial observance we are instructed to symbolically partake of the bread (His body) and the cup (His blood) in remembrance with sincere thankfulness, serious self-examination, and brotherly love until He comes.

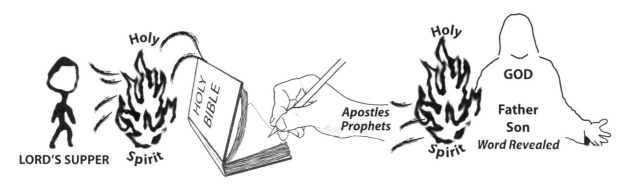

Observation: Read and observe the following verses and write down what you learn about the Lord's Supper.

Example: 1 Timothy 3:14-15 _Paul writes to Timothy on how <u>one ought to behave</u> in the <u>household of God,</u> which is the <u>church of the living God,</u> a pillar and buttress of truth._

Exodus 12:1-30 _____

_____

_____

Matthew 26:17-30 _____

_____

Mark 14:22-26 _____

_____

Luke 22:7-20 _____

_____

_____

Acts 2:42-47 _____

_____

Acts 20:7, 11 _____

_____

_____

1 Corinthians 11:17-35 _____

_____

Revelation 3:15-20 _____

_____

_____

Respond: Based on these verses, write a brief summary of the key principles and functions that you observed from God's Word that every person, family and church could follow at any time, in any culture. (Absolutes) _____

_____

_____

_____

Discussion: Contrast these principles with your life, family and church experience today.

_____

_____

_____

_____

What changes do you need to make in your life, family and church here and now? _____

_____

_____

_____

_____

Application: How and when will you make these changes in your life, family and church?

_____

_____

_____

_____

Biblical Issues in the Church Family

Lesson 56
Spiritual Gifts

The Word of God describes spiritual gifts as a special ability given freely by the Holy Spirit to every believer at their conversion. This gift of grace is for the purpose of building up the church family and the Body of Christ. Each person should minister interdependently with one another in love.

Observation: Read and observe the following verses and write down what you learn about spiritual gifts.

Example: 1 Timothy 3:14-15 <u>Paul writes to Timothy on how <u>one ought to behave</u> in the <u>household</u> of God,</u> which is the <u>church of the living God,</u> a pillar and buttress of truth.

Romans 11:29 _____
_____
_____

Romans 12:1-8 _____
_____
_____

1 Corinthians 7:7 _____
_____

1 Corinthians 12:1 _____
_____

1 Corinthians 12–14 _____
_____

Ephesians 4:1-16 _____

_____

_____

1 Timothy 4:14 _____

_____

_____

1 Peter 4:7-11 _____

_____

_____

Respond: Based on these verses, write a brief summary of the key principles and functions that you observed from God's Word that every person, family and church could follow at any time, in any culture. (Absolutes) _____

_____

_____

_____

Discussion: Contrast these principles with your life, family and church experience today.

_____

_____

_____

_____

What changes do you need to make in your life, family and church here and now? _____

_____

_____

_____

_____

Application: How and when will you make these changes in your life, family and church?

_____

_____

_____

_____

Lesson 57
Giving and Financial Matters

The Word of God is clear that everything belongs to God but He has entrusted his people with some of it. He expects us to discharge our stewardship wisely and faithfully, but first we are to give our hearts to Christ. Giving is proof of our love for Christ. We cannot love without giving.

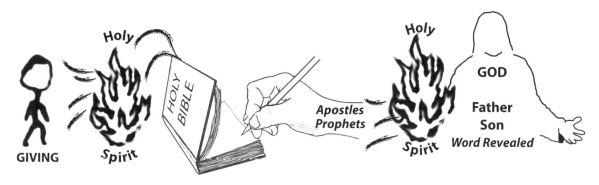

Observation: Read and observe the following verses and write down what you learn about giving and money.

Example: 1 Timothy 3:14-15 _Paul writes to Timothy on how <u>one ought to behave</u> in the <u>household</u> <u>of God,</u> which is the <u>church of the living God,</u> a pillar and buttress of truth._

Matthew 6:19-21 _____

_____

_____

Matthew 14:13-21 _____

_____

_____

Luke 21:1-4 _____

_____

Acts 6:1-7 _____

_____

Acts 11:27-30 _____

_____

Acts 20:35 _____

_____

Galatians 6:6-10 _____

_____

2 Thessalonians 3:6-15 _____

_____

1 Corinthians 16:1-4 _____

_____

2 Corinthians 8:1–9:15 _____

_____

1 Timothy 3:3-5 _____

_____

1 Timothy 5:1-18 _____

_____

Respond: Based on these verses, write a brief summary of the key principles and functions that you observed from God's Word that every person, family and church could follow at any time, in any culture. (Absolutes) _____

_____

_____

Discussion: Contrast these principles with your life, family and church experience today.

_____

_____

_____

What changes do you need to make in your life, family and church here and now? _____

_____

_____

Application: How and when will you make these changes in your life, family and church?

_____

_____

_____

Biblical Issues in the Church Family

Lesson 58
Strong and the Weak

Today, most divisions in the body of Christ are caused by non-absolutes (forms and traditions). The Word of God teaches how to disagree on non-absolutes and still maintain unity. This is accomplished by accepting and loving one another as Christ has accepted and loved you.

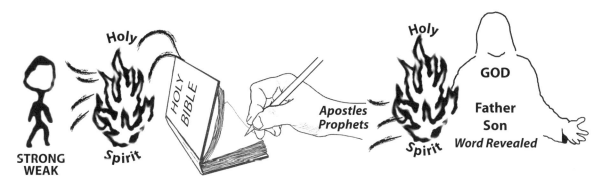

Observation: Read and observe the following verses and write down what you learn about the strong and the weak.

Example: 1 Timothy 3:14-15 *Paul writes to Timothy on how <u>one ought to behave</u> in the <u>household of God,</u> which is the <u>church of the living God,</u> a pillar and buttress of truth.*

Romans 14:1-3 _____

_____

Romans 14:5 _____

_____

Romans 14:6-7 _____   _____

_____

Romans 14:8-10 _____

_____

Romans 14:13 _____

_____

Romans 14:14-15 _____

_____

Romans 14:16-20 _____

_____

Romans 14:21-22 _____

_____

Romans 15:1-7 _____

_____

1 Corinthians 10:23-24 _____

_____

1 Corinthians 10:25-29 _____

_____

1 Corinthians 13 _____

_____

Respond: Based on these verses, write a brief summary of the key principles and functions that you observed from God's Word that every person, family and church could follow at any time, in any culture. (Absolutes) _____

_____

_____

Discussion: Contrast these principles with your life, family and church experience today.

_____

_____

_____

What changes do you need to make in your life, family and church here and now? _____

_____

_____

_____

Application: How and when will you make these changes in your life, family and church?

_____

_____

_____

Biblical Issues in the Church Family

Lesson 59
Roles of Men and Women

Today's culture has redefined the roles of men and women in the family and the church into a model that is contrary to the Word of God. As you hear God speak, you will observe the sacred beauty of God's design for men and women within the family and church.

Observation: Read and observe the following verses and write down what you learn about the roles of men and women.

Example: 1 Timothy 3:14-15 _Paul writes to Timothy on how <u>one ought to behave</u> in the <u>household of God,</u> which is the <u>church of the living God,</u> a pillar and buttress of truth._

Luke 2:36-38 _____

_____

Acts 1:14 _____

_____

Acts 2:17; 21:9 _____

_____

Galatians 3:28 _____

_____

1 Corinthians 11:1-16 _____

_____

_____

1 Corinthians 14:26-40 _____

_____

Ephesians 5:21–6:4 _____

_____

Colossians 3:18–4:1 _____

_____

1 Timothy 2:8-14 _____

_____

1 Timothy 3:4-5 _____

_____

1 Timothy 5:9-15 _____

_____

Titus 2:3-5 _____

_____

Respond: Based on these verses, write a brief summary of the key principles and functions that you observed from God's Word that every person, family and church could follow at any time, in any culture. (Absolutes) _____

_____

_____

Discussion: Contrast these principles with your life, family and church experience today.

_____

_____

What changes do you need to make in your life, family and church here and now? _____

_____

_____

Application: How and when will you make these changes in your life, family and church?

_____

_____

_____

_____

Biblical Issues in the Church Family

Lesson 60
Employer and Employee Relationship

Some Bible translations refer to the employer and employee relationship as a master and slave relationship. The church today often separates work relationships in the market place as unsacred and not as important as ministry but the New Testament makes no distinction. Paul considered his tentmaking relationships and work an important ministry and opportunity to show Christ.

Observation: Read and observe the following verses and write down what you learn about the relationship between Employers and Employees.

Example: 1 Timothy 3:14-15 _Paul writes to Timothy on how one ought to behave in the household of God, which is the church of the living God, a pillar and buttress of truth._

Ephesians 6:5-9 _____

_____

_____

Colossians 3:17 4:2 _____

_____

_____

1 Timothy 6:1-3 _____

_____

_____

Titus 2:7-10 _____

_____

_____

Philemon _____

_____

_____

I Peter 2:16-25 _____

_____

_____

Respond: Based on these verses, write a brief summary of the key principles and functions that you observed from God's Word that every person, family and church could follow at any time, in any culture. (Absolutes) _____

_____

_____

_____

Discussion: Contrast these principles with your life, family and church experience today.

_____

_____

_____

_____

What changes do you need to make in your life, family and church here and now? _____

_____

_____

_____

_____

Application: How and when will you make these changes in your life, family and church?

_____

_____

_____

_____

Biblical Issues in the Church Family

Lesson 61
Questionable Things (Should I or should I not?)

The Word of God distinguishes between moral absolutes and non-absolutes. One must make up his/her own mind under the Holy Spirit's leading in matters of biblical non-absolutes. Remember, love must rule our freedom and personal preferences should not be imposed on others.

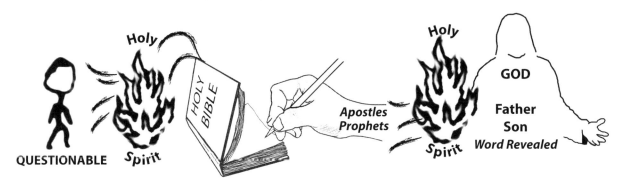

Observation: Read and observe the following verses and write down what you learn about questionable things.

Example: 1 Timothy 3:14-15 _Paul writes to Timothy on how <u>one ought to behave</u> in the <u>household</u>_ <u>of God,</u> which is the <u>church of the living God,</u> a pillar and buttress of truth.

Matthew 18:6-7 _____

_____

Romans 14:5, 14, 23 _____

_____

Romans 14:6-8 _____

_____

Romans 14:13, 15, 20-21 _____

_____

Romans 14:17-18 _____

_____

Romans 14:19 _____

_____

Romans 14:22 _____

_____

1 Corinthians 6:12-20 _____

_____

1 Corinthians 8:9-13 _____

_____

1 Corinthians 10:31 _____

_____

I Peter 2:16-21 _____

_____

1 John 2:3-6 _____

_____

Respond: Based on these verses, write a brief summary of the key principles and functions that you observed from God's Word that every person, family and church could follow at any time, in any culture. (Absolutes) _____

_____

_____

Discussion: Contrast these principles with your life, family and church experience today.

_____

_____

_____

_____

What changes do you need to make in your life, family and church here and now? _____

_____

_____

_____

Application: How and when will you make these changes in your life, family and church?

_____

_____

_____

Biblical Issues in the Church Family

Lesson 62
Fasting

Many people in the Bible fasted; Moses, Hannah, David, and the entire nation of Israel fasted on the Day of Atonement. Fasting was not just an Old Testament practice because Jesus, Anna, Paul and the Antioch Church fasted. Fasting is a form or non-absolute which provides an opportunity to search one's heart, pray and repent as long as it is done for the glory of God.

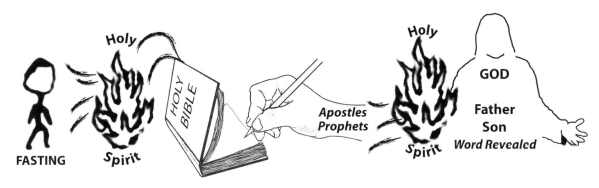

Observation: Read and observe the following verses and write down what you learn about fasting.

Example: 1 Timothy 3:14-15 <u>Paul writes to Timothy on how one ought to behave in the household of God,</u> which is the <u>church of the living God,</u> a pillar and buttress of truth.

Judges 20:26-28 _____

_____

I Samuel 1:1–2:11 _____

_____

Ezra 8:21-23 _____

_____

Esther 4:12-17 _____

_____

Psalm 35:13 _____

_____

Isaiah 58:1-14 _____

_____

Joel 2:12-13 _____

_____

Matthew 4:1-11 _____

_____

Matthew 6:16-18 _____

_____

Luke 5:33-35 _____

_____

Acts 13:2-3 _____

_____

I Corinthians 7:4-5 _____

_____

Respond: Based on these verses, write a brief summary of the key principles and functions that you observed from God's Word that every person, family and church could follow at any time, in any culture. (Absolutes) _____

_____

_____

Discussion: Contrast these principles with your life, family and church experience today.

_____

_____

_____

What changes do you need to make in your life, family and church here and now? _____

_____

_____

_____

Application: How and when will you make these changes in your life, family and church?

_____

_____

_____

_____

Lesson 63
Relationship with the World and Government

The Word of God speaks clearly about your relationship with the world and its governments. The church is to obey and respect the governing authorities. Believers are called to present their bodies as living sacrifices and not to reform or conform to the world but to be transformed. Jesus, Paul and the early apostles set an excellent example of our relationship with the world.

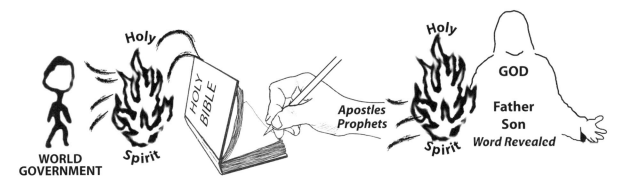

Observation: Read and observe the following verses and write down what you learn about the world and government.

Example: 1 Timothy 3:14-15 *Paul writes to Timothy on how one ought to behave in the household of God, which is the church of the living God, a pillar and buttress of truth.*

Matthew 5:13-16 _____

_____

John 15:17-20 _____

_____

Acts 5:24-29 _____

_____

Romans 12:1-2 _____

_____

Romans 13:1-7 _____

_____

Ephesians 3:8-11 _____

_____

Ephesians 6:10-20 _____

_____

Colossians 4:2-6 _____

_____

1 Timothy 2:1-8 _____

_____

Titus 2:1-15 _____

_____

Titus 3:1-14 _____

_____

1 John 2:15-17 _____

_____

Respond: Based on these verses, write a brief summary of the key principles and functions that you observed from God's Word that every person, family and church could follow at any time, in any culture. (Absolutes) _____

_____

_____

Discussion: Contrast these principles with your life, family and church experience today.

_____

_____

_____

What changes do you need to make in your life, family and church here and now? _____

_____

_____

Application: How and when will you make these changes in your life, family and church?

_____

_____

_____

Biblical Issues in the Church Family

Project L
Keeping the Church in Order

1. Write the biblical guidelines for each of the 17 *Biblical Issues in the Church Family* lessons and their implications for today (Lessons 47–63).

God's Word _____
_____

Hearing God _____
_____

Servant Leaders _____
_____

Spirit Baptism _____
_____

Water Baptism _____
_____

Church Membership _____
_____

Resolving Conflict _____
_____

Assembly Meetings _____
_____

Lord's Supper _____
_____

Spiritual Gifts _____
_____

Giving _____

_____

Strong and Weak Believers _____

_____

Roles of Men and Women _____

_____

Employer/Employee Relationship _____

_____

Questionable Things _____

_____

Fasting _____

_____

Relationship with World _____

_____

2. Compare your church with your outline (above). Where does your church need to change?

_____

_____

_____

3. What can you do to help make that happen? _____

_____

_____

_____

4. Write a brief strategy of your role and responsibility in your church family. _____

_____

_____

_____

_____

Review Chapters 1, 2, 3, 4, 5, and 6 before going to 7.

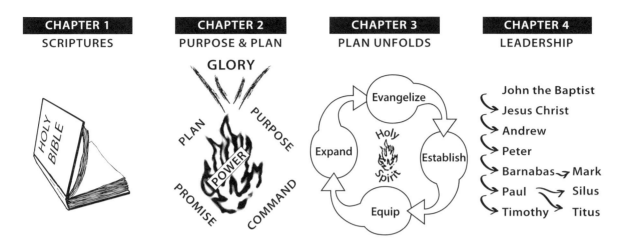

CHAPTER 1	CHAPTER 2	CHAPTER 3	CHAPTER 4
SCRIPTURES	PURPOSE & PLAN	PLAN UNFOLDS	LEADERSHIP

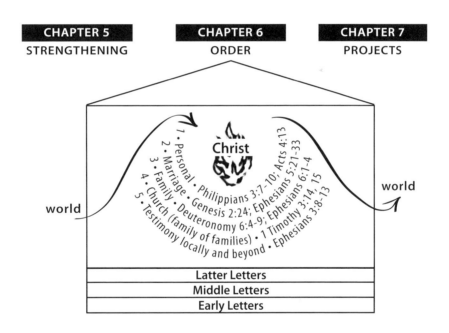

CHAPTER 5	CHAPTER 6	CHAPTER 7
STRENGTHENING	ORDER	PROJECTS

OUR CHALLENGE

Develop a Church Planting and Renewal Strategy

Our Challenge: Now we want to take all that we have learned from God's Word and develop a Church Planting and Renewal Strategy but first let us review again. See if you can fill in the blanks in the diagram on the next page without looking back:

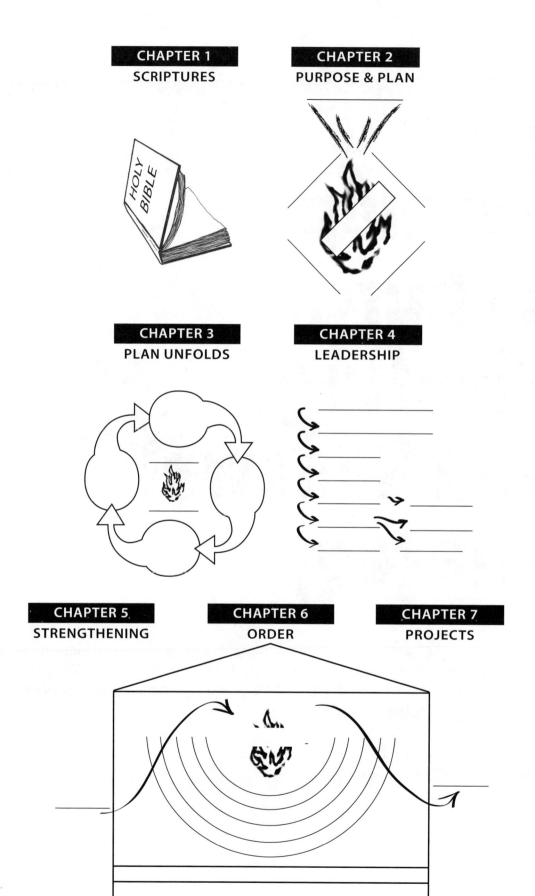

CHAPTER 1
SCRIPTURES

CHAPTER 2
PURPOSE & PLAN

CHAPTER 3
PLAN UNFOLDS

CHAPTER 4
LEADERSHIP

CHAPTER 5
STRENGTHENING

CHAPTER 6
ORDER

CHAPTER 7
PROJECTS

Project M
Design Your Own Church Planting and Renewal Strategy

Use Supra-Cultural Timeless Principles to Connect the "Then" with your "Now." To help you understand look at the following diagram again:

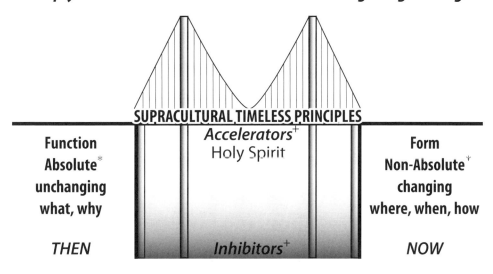

First, let's review *Absolutes and Non-Absolutes on pages 54-55 and +Accelerators and Inhibitors on pages 22-24. Now, using the timeless and supra-cultural principles outlined below that we have studied from the Bible, design a strategy for fully establishing a church from start to finish in your situation and culture.

I. Church Evangelizing

A. Being Sent

1. _____
   _____

2. _____
   _____

3. _____
   _____

4. _____
   _____

B. Proclaiming the Gospel

    1. _____
    _____

    2. _____
    _____

    3. _____
    _____

    4. _____
    _____

C. Baptizing Believers

    1. _____
    _____

    2. _____
    _____

II. Church Establishing

A. In the Gospel of Faith

    1. _____
    _____

    2. _____
    _____

    3. _____
    _____

    4. _____
    _____

B. Ordered Households

    1. _____
    _____

    2. _____
    _____

3. _____
   _____

4. _____
   _____

C. Faithful Men

   1. _____
      _____

   2. _____
      _____

   3. _____
      _____

   4. _____
      _____

III. Church Equipping

A. Men

   1. _____
      _____

   2. _____
      _____

   3. _____
      _____

   4. _____
      _____

B. Women

   1. _____
      _____

   2. _____
      _____

   3. _____
      _____

4. _____

C. Children

1. _____

2. _____

3. _____

4. _____

IV. Church Expanding

A. Locally

1. _____

2. _____

3. _____

4. _____

B. Other Nations (people groups)

1. _____

2. _____

3. _____

4. _____

Project N
10-Year Church Planting and Church Renewal Strategy

Using your new personal "Church Planting and Renewal Strategy" develop and chart a ten-year chronological and geographical strategy. If applicable you can add people groups in your strategy. Refer to the Antioch Model cycle below as a guideline. Of course, this strategy is subject to the authority of Christ, who is Head of the Church, and in the freedom of the Holy Spirit's direction. As you know, the Holy Spirit would often change Paul's strategic plans. Your strategy will reflect the outline from Project M, pages 231-234. Page 236 is for you to chart your ten-year church planting and/or church renewal strategy. At top is a map of the progress of the early church you can use as a guideline. Of course the places and dates will change.

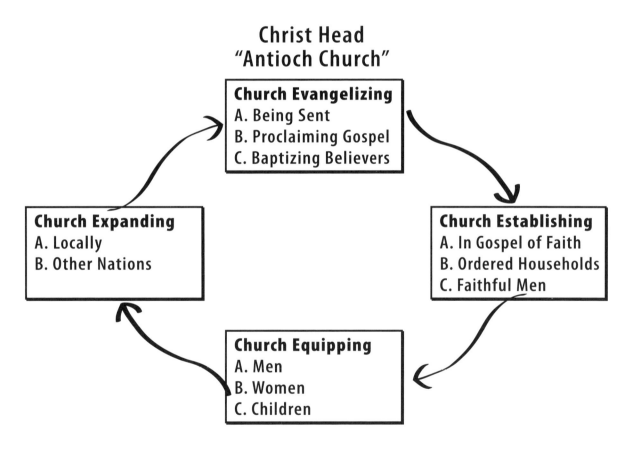

**Christ Head
"Antioch Church"**

Church Evangelizing
A. Being Sent
B. Proclaiming Gospel
C. Baptizing Believers

Church Establishing
A. In Gospel of Faith
B. Ordered Households
C. Faithful Men

Church Equipping
A. Men
B. Women
C. Children

Church Expanding
A. Locally
B. Other Nations

Chart your ten-year church planting and/or renewal strategy.

Using the top map's locations and dates as a guideline, chart your ten-year church planting and/or renewal strategy by filling in the blank map at the bottom of this page.

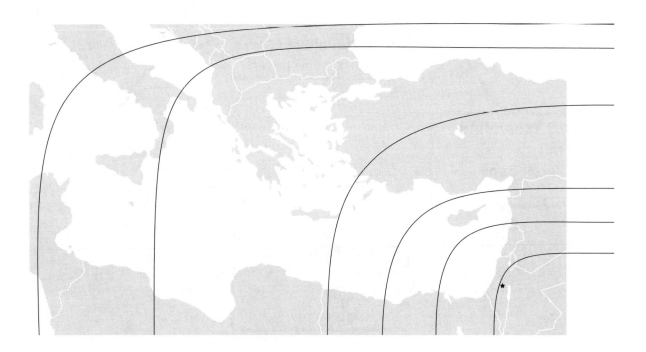

Below are two simplified skeleton outlines, one for starting new churches and one for renewing and establishing existing churches.

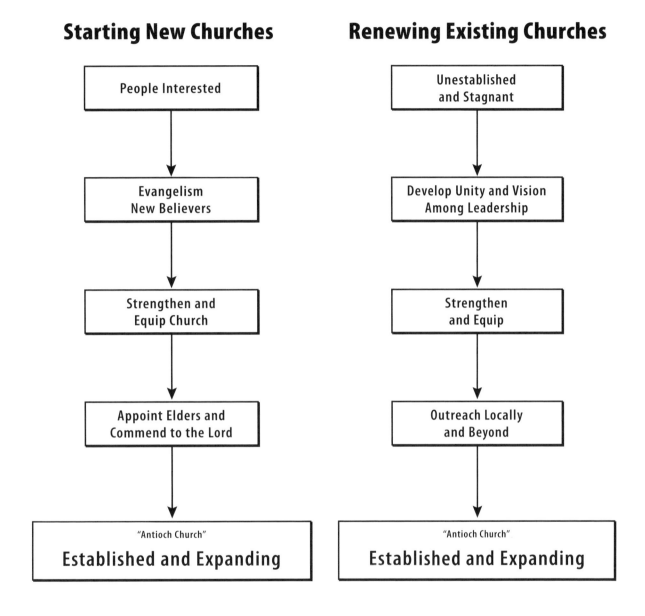

Starting New Churches

People Interested

↓

Evangelism
New Believers

↓

Strengthen and
Equip Church

↓

Appoint Elders and
Commend to the Lord

↓

"Antioch Church"
Established and Expanding

Renewing Existing Churches

Unestablished
and Stagnant

↓

Develop Unity and Vision
Among Leadership

↓

Strengthen
and Equip

↓

Outreach Locally
and Beyond

↓

"Antioch Church"
Established and Expanding

Project O
Apostle's Ministry Assessment

The following assessment should be evaluated annually, independently and with your other church leaders. Although no ministry is perfect in every area, there should be steady progress in the areas you are dissatisfied with. Circle the number that expresses your assessment below.

Preaching (Acts 11:19-20) Christians scattered, preaching the gospel

Dissatisfied   1   2   3   4   5   6   7   Satisfied

Turning (Acts 11:21) Many turned to the Lord

Dissatisfied   1   2   3   4   5   6   7   Satisfied

Sending (Acts 11:22-24a) Jerusalem Church sends Barnabas to Antioch

Dissatisfied   1   2   3   4   5   6   7   Satisfied

Multiplying (Acts 11:24b) Antioch Church adds a great number of people to the Lord

Dissatisfied   1   2   3   4   5   6   7   Satisfied

Discipling (Acts 11:25) Barnabas gets Saul's help

Dissatisfied   1   2   3   4   5   6   7   Satisfied

Teaching (Acts 11:26) Barnabas and Saul taught a great many people for a year

Dissatisfied   1   2   3   4   5   6   7   Satisfied

Maturing (Acts 11:26) Believers were first called Christians in Antioch

Dissatisfied   1   2   3   4   5   6   7   Satisfied

Sending and Reproducing (Acts 13:1-4) Antioch Church sends Barnabas and Saul to the world

Dissatisfied   1   2   3   4   5   6   7   Satisfied

Evangelizing (Acts 13:4–14:21) They evangelized strategic cities

Dissatisfied   1   2   3   4   5   6   7   Satisfied

Instructing (Acts 14:21-22) Instructed the new believers

Dissatisfied   1   2   3   4   5   6   7   Satisfied

Appointing (Acts 14:23) Appointed Elders

Dissatisfied   1   2   3   4   5   6   7   Satisfied

Accountability (Acts 14:27-28) They reported to Antioch

Dissatisfied   1   2   3   4   5   6   7   Satisfied

Establishing (Acts 15:36–28:31 and the Epistles) They established churches by visits and letters

Dissatisfied   1   2   3   4   5   6   7   Satisfied

Teamwork (Acts) They networked with missionary teams and with churches

Dissatisfied   1   2   3   4   5   6   7   Satisfied

Equipping (2 Corinthians 2:12-13) They gave priority to a struggling church over an opened door

Dissatisfied   1   2   3   4   5   6   7   Satisfied

Fulfilled (Romans 15:19-20) The gospel was preached from Jerusalem to Illyricum

Dissatisfied   1   2   3   4   5   6   7   Satisfied

Expanding (Acts 28:30-31) The gospel continued to expand

Dissatisfied   1   2   3   4   5   6   7   Satisfied

Baton Passed (2 Timothy 2:2ff) The next generation of leaders continued the process

Dissatisfied   1   2   3   4   5   6   7   Satisfied

Discussion Questions: Why are most churches today not making this kind of progress like they did in the early church? _____

_____

_____

_____

What functions above are you dissatisfied with and how can you help measure up biblically?

_____

_____

_____

_____